D0560533

GOD KNOWS WHO I AM

Seeing Yourself as He Sees You

Guideposts®

CARMEL, NEW YORK 10512

www.guidepostsbooks.com

www.guidepostsbooks.com
Guideposts Book & Inspirational Media Division

Compiled by Marie Gangemi
Designed by Bob Antler, Antler Designworks

CONTENTS

INTRODUCTION
Eric Fellman

Some of the most comforting, and terrifying, words in the Scriptures are found in Psalm 139:

"O Lord, you have searched me and you know me. You know when I sit and when I rise; you perceive my thoughts from afar. You discern my going out and my lying down; you are familiar with all my ways. Before a word is on my tongue you know it completely, O Lord." (vs. 1-4)

God knows me, and He knows you. He knows us so fully that the Psalmist says he "knit" us together while we were still in our mother's womb. The frightening thing is all my fears, angers, corrupt thoughts and jealous envies are fully known to God. That alone could make me feel desolate and forsaken; who would want such a jumble of contradictory selfishness? Except that God says he sees all these things and loves me completely, even with my faults.

I learned a little about this love a couple of years ago when God allowed me to be a reflection of this type of love for one of my sons. Jason, our oldest, was off to college in Vermont and got himself knotted up into some bad situations. His grades had faltered, he dropped classes and was falling behind on his graduation schedule. After a night of too much partying the car he was riding in was wrecked, no one was badly hurt, but all were shook up. And his involvement with a young lady became so tangled that he felt trapped and alone.

All these were things we had talked about and most of the specifics I had anticipated and strongly warned him against, but he went ahead anyway. I was a stern father, with high standards and, in his mind, an unforgiving one. Kind of like many of us view God, I guess.

Then one night Jason reached the end of his rope and called home at 1 A.M. The phone rang. My wife Joy picked it up and he asked to speak to me. He told me all that had gone wrong, and then tearfully asked, "Dad, could I just come home?"

Instantly, I wanted to reply, "What, drop out in the middle of a semester when you are already behind? Get your act together, kid."

However, the Lord allowed me to breathe a prayer before saying anything, and in that moment He showed me some of the dumb things I had done in life. And he also let me hear my son's crying. Suddenly I knew he was crying and fearful that I would say "no" and, more than anything else, he needed to be loved. I found myself crying and saying, "Of course you can come home, Jason, I'm just sorry you thought I would say, 'no'." That very morning I got in my car and drove up to get him. A few months at home cleared his perspective and he returned to finish and head off into life with a vibrant confidence.

Admit it, you usually think God has a reaction similar to my first one to Jason. Somewhere in the back of your mind you hear him saying, "What! You can't be serious, get your act together!"

You see, God knows us completely, yet his first and always response to us is love. No matter what we think of ourselves, he loves us. The biggest mistake many of us make in life is to look for love everywhere else but in the arms of our Heavenly father.

As we celebrated our 26th wedding anniversary this year, our middle son Nathan was teasing me one night that "they just don't make them like Mom anymore, Dad, you are the luckiest guy in the world." Knowing his penchant for visiting the clubs around Washington, D.C. and the resulting unattached nature of his current relationships, I replied, "Well Nathan, maybe you're looking for love in the wrong places, I found your Mom in church."

Sometimes we are like that, we seek out love everywhere but where it is seeking us, in the heart of God. We're sort of like the bumblebee that flew into my tent on a camping trip this past summer. I'd left the front opening unzipped and the whole back side was a screen window that had the rain-fly open. The bee flew straight in and headed for what looked like a wide opening at the back. Then he ran into the screen. Wildly he threw him- self at the screen, bouncing across the length and breadth of the window. Desperately he tried to get out, when all he needed to do was turn around and go back the way he came. Furiously, compulsively he banged against the screen until nearly exhausted. Finally I was able to scoop him onto a piece of paper and show him the way out.

The open door that is always there for us is the love of God. No one put it better than the Apostle John who wrote:

This is how God showed his great love among us: He sent his one and only Son into the world that we might live through him. This is love: not that we loved God, but that he loved us… I John 4:9

We're like that bee when we flail away at parts of life that can never satisfy. We become workaholics, alcoholics, and very often, foodaholics. We work ourselves to exhaustion and never find the way out to freedom to be ourselves in the world He has created for us. The way out is to come home to his love, to be healed in his presence and then to return to the world and share His love through our actions to others who are desperately seeking for something they can't quite define.

Jesus gave us clear direction on this path when he was asked, "what is the greatest commandment?" His reply was:

"Love the Lord your God with all your heart and with all your soul and with all your mind and with all your strength. The second is this: 'Love your neighbor as yourself'."

Loving God and loving our neighbor starts with loving ourselves and this is the key to freedom from every compulsion and addiction. Read this book with excitement for the many ways God knows you and loves you. It will lead you to the same conclusion the Psalmist reached in the passage where we began, and there is immense power in this conclusion:

Search me O God and know my heart; test me and know my anxious thoughts. See if there is any offensive way in me, and lead me in the way everlasting. Psalm 139:23-24.

LOOKING WITH LOVE
❧❀❧

God's love is the greatest gift to us. It is hard to fathom the extent of it and because we are only human beings, such understanding may be impossible. It is nearly as difficult to understand human love—romantic, brotherly, for children, for friends—it is a gift for the recipient and the donor. Yet we can give that gift and receive it when we open our hearts to God.

As you read the following selections, you'll see how love transforms the viewer and the viewed…and makes "wrinkles" turn into "twinkles."

A friend loveth at all times.

—PROVERBS 17:17

FOR SPECIAL PEOPLE

Lord, I want to pause today and thank You
for the blessing of people in my life
who are willing to be vulnerable and open;
who are willing to accept me as I am,
who are willing to question me when I am wrong
and gently point me back to You.
Thank You for allowing them to love me
through Your power

—Dolphus Weary

I will praise thee; for I am fearfully and wonderfully made. . . .
—Psalm 139:14

All my life I've felt self-conscious about my teeth. You see, they're crooked. When I was a child, my parents could not afford to have them straightened, and after Larry and I got married, we couldn't afford it either. Now whenever I look in a mirror, I see graying hair, trifocal glasses, wrinkles, . . . and crooked teeth.

Recently, two of our son's young daughters came to visit us for the weekend. On Saturday morning, six-year-old Cheyanne looked up from her bowl of breakfast cereal and said to me, "Grandma, you're so nice and you're so pretty. When I grow up, I want to be like you and look like you."

Caught up in my old insecurity, I replied, "Oh, no, Cheyanne, I'm not pretty, not with these crooked teeth. But I'm glad you love me anyway."

I guess she must have brooded about this all day, for at bedtime she turned to me suddenly and said in a fierce voice, "Grandma, you *are* pretty! And so are your teeth!"

My granddaughter's forthrightness jolted me. But it was the most heartwarming compliment I've ever received. For the first time in a long time, I really *did* feel beautiful, and I hugged her and told her so.

Nowadays I try to remember the wisdom a six-year-old passed on to me: Seen through a filter of love, all people are beautiful.

Father, I praise You for the wondrous gift You've given us, the eyes of love.
—Madge Harrah

In every thing give thanks: for this is the will of God. . . .
—I Thessalonians 5:18

It really was about time we bought some new furniture. The old bookshelves sagged under the weight of volumes, the TV cabinet doors never closed, our dinner table wobbled whenever the boys used it for coloring, the chairs had flaking paint. And yet. . . .

"We couldn't replace the table," my wife said. "It always reminds me of Rodney. He gave it to us when he moved out of the city, and I like keeping it in hopes that he'll move back."

"And the bookshelf," I acknowledged. "Nancy and Dominic gave it to us when they had their first child, when their 'office' became a nursery. It reminds me of them."

"The end table has to stay," Carol said. I nodded. An elderly neighbor gave it to us before moving to a nursing home.

"Your dad bought us the TV cabinet when we first moved here," I said.

"The chairs came from your parents' basement," my wife added. "We didn't think we'd need them for long, but it's been eight years now."

"Nine," I corrected. "They've been more permanent than we knew."

"There isn't anything I'd like to get rid of," Carol finally said. "So what if we don't have an apartment where everything matches. We've got something better."

"What's that?" I asked.

"A home," she said, "that makes us think of those who helped us make it one."

Lord, I'm thankful for a life that isn't store-bought.
—Rick Hamlin

Marvelous are thy works; and that my soul knoweth right well.
My substance was not hid from thee. . . . —Psalm 139:14-15

🍂 I am short. And it bothers me. My children laugh at me, now that they are all at least four inches taller than I. "Shortie, shortie, Mom," they tease affectionately.

Many years ago I went to boarding school in England. Every day for the nine years I spent there, my class marched in line into morning prayer, tallest first, down to shortest last. And I was always the last. All those years in school I'd hear in my head Jesus' words from the Sermon on the Mount, "Which of you by taking thought can add one cubit unto his stature?" (Matthew 6:27), and wished I could prove Him wrong somehow!

When I came to live in the United States, things got better. The nations represented here include enough people who are naturally small that I stopped feeling self-conscious. I still wanted to wear long, slim dresses and to be able to see across a crowded room to find a friendly face.

I worry about my height, even though I know it's foolish. Then one day I was walking to lunch with an old friend, and she admired an elegant cape in a department store window. "What a great color," she said. "It would really suit you."

"Oh, I couldn't wear that," I replied. "I'm too short."

"Really?" she said in surprise. "How tall are you? I've never thought of you as short."

What a moment! I realized that I had quite missed the point of those words in Matthew. Here on a crowded city sidewalk, by taking thought, my friend had added much more than a cubit to my stature. She had changed my self-perception.

God, I accept the body You've given me. Help me to treat it with respect.   —Brigitte Weeks

13

And forget not all his benefits. —*Psalm* 103:2

As my husband and I were traveling through the southern part of Illinois on our way home from vacation, we stopped for breakfast in a truckers' café. While we were waiting our turn at the cashier's stand, my ears tuned in as an older man greeted a young woman with, "How are you *mostly?"*

When we got back into the car I told Ken what I had heard, and we discussed how we would have answered for ourselves. We were tired and dreaded getting back into harness after vacation. We had some aches and pains. We were concerned about my mother and some problems our children face.

But *mostly,* we decided, we were fine! God loved us. We loved each other. We had challenging work to do. We were members of a church that cared. We had shelter, food, clothing, and a car that ran. And even with the aches and pains, we could function.

How are you mostly? Remember, *mostly* is what counts!

Dear Lord, help me to take time to remember Your blessings.
—*Barbara Chafin*

There are diversities of operations, but it is the same God which worketh all in all. . . . —*I Corinthians* 12:6

While visiting the Smithsonian's Museum of Natural History in Washington, D.C. I found a display of aragonite, a form of calcium carbonate, that was particularly intriguing. There were several forms of aragonite shown, each different, yet with the same atomic structure. One form consisted of milky spearlike crystals, while another was composed of opaque white strands that looked like chow mein noodles. The same mineral, the same atomic structure, yet depending upon their environment, very different appearances. Obviously, there is no one ideal form in which aragonite must appear.

I used to struggle to be neat and tidy, thinking that "neat" was ideal and "cluttered" was somehow wrong. I'd spend hours cleaning closets, organizing desk drawers, and clearing off tabletops, only to feel guilty when they became cluttered again A friend pointed out to me that my way of doing things–cluttered and untidy–wasn't wrong, just different.

It's not that I'm a slob, because order and cleanliness *are* important. But I don't have to live by someone else's standard of organization. I can accept that my clutter makes sense for *my* needs and allows me to relax.

The New Testament says that God has created each of us different, like those varieties of aragonite. We each have our own traits, our own "glory" like the sun, moon, and stars (I Corinthians 15:41).

Instead of worrying about clutter, I can read, or have quiet time with God, or play soccer with my boys. And I think that's just what my loving Creator intended .

Creator God, let me take time to rejoice in my uniqueness today, knowing that You created me exactly as I was meant to be. Amen. —*Lisa Isenhower*

Love is the fulfilling of the law. —Romans 13:10

In the latter part of the 19th century, a devout young Quaker named Annie Barrow lived in a town called Kendal, in the English midlands. One day she went to an elder in her church to ask for prayer. "I fear," she told him, "that I have no talent at all for serving God!"

The elder studied her for a moment and replied, "Methinks thou hast a talent for loving!"

Apparently he was right. Annie eventually married a young man who became one of the great commissioners of the Salvation Army, and Annie herself became the legendary matriarch of several generations of devoted Christian missionaries, preachers, doctors, nurses, and teachers who have wrapped themselves around the globe like the Savior's arms, helping, healing, comforting, serving, and above all, loving.

I think of Annie Barrow when I'm in one of my "worthless me" moods. I get this way when I'm sick or exhausted from overworking, and right now I'm in the throes of an illness that will probably require major surgery. I don't like being out of commission. *What good am I,* I ask myself, *when I can't work? When I can't contribute?* I try to remind myself, at times like this, that God doesn't measure me only according to my works.

That's when I open my Bible and find this little story about Annie Barrow inside the cover. I'm reminded that "a talent for loving" has been given to everyone–including me–and that I can find ways to use it no matter how I feel, no matter where I am. Even in a hospital bed or right here at home.

Father, today I will use my "talent for loving" with everyone You send my way. —Susan Williams

But God is faithful, who will not suffer you to be tempted above that ye are able. . . .   —I Corinthians 10:13

In *Now or Never*, a book by the late Dr. Smiley Blanton, the renowned psychiatrist says that everyone is fighting a demon. Some have learned to control it, others have learned to live with it, but no one has eliminated it. The demon is anxiety. Some call it worry.

I have it, too. For years, I worried about a paycheck. I was concerned about health although mine was excellent. And there were others that I concealed and denied. Being black, would I be courteously received at a department store? Would I be served at a restaurant? Would I be welcomed at a church of my faith in a strange city? If I accepted an upgrade, would coworkers accept me? These worries plagued me long after laws and attitudes were changed.

Then, one day at lunch, a friend said, "Oscar, I don't understand you. You never let anyone get close to you. Even your wife speaks of this. Don't you trust people?"

The words tore through my armor. The truth was I didn't trust anyone–even myself. To conceal this, I acted as if I didn't need others. It was hard to change now, but I shared my feelings with my friend who listened and hugged me. Later I tried joining various groups and volunteered at a community center. People welcomed my company, and I was delighted over my new sharing with my new "family." I learned that others needed reassurances, too.

Dr. Blanton said that the demon can never be eliminated. But knowing where the demon lies helps to overcome it. My friend helped me, and I helped others. You can, too.

Lord, worry is my lack of trust and faith. Teach me to work at it, and forgive me when I stumble.   —Oscar Greene

Ye should show forth the praises of him who hath called you out of darkness into his marvelous light.   —I Peter 2:9

🍂 Living in the country is a new adventure for me. One evening, I noticed a small, black fur ball moving through our yard. I approached cautiously. It was a baby skunk! I spotted another and still another. In all, six baby skunks that had somehow been orphaned greeted me.

I brought out a can of cat food and the visitors quickly gathered around. I discovered that they lived under our house in a deep dark hole. A vet instructed me how to move their food out farther from the house each time I fed them until they discovered the woods—and freedom.

I always marveled at their trust as they waddled and tumbled out of their dark hole, one by one. Spooning out cat food, I remembered a deep, dark hole of self-pity I'd found myself in after I'd become a widow. Although four years had gone by, I mostly kept to myself. One night, feeling so alone, I poked my head out of my hole and called some friends. Almost trembling, I asked if I could join them. I was so surprised when they all exclaimed, "Yes, yes! We'll come and get you. We love you!" Tears of gratitude had prevented me from saying anything except "'bye."

Maybe you've been "hiding" for your own reasons and are ready to come out. Take a deep breath, and with a prayer and God's courage, take that first step. Call a friend who's been waiting patiently. Send in the application for that new job. Volunteer to lead a church group. Start by trusting God.

When I am afraid, Lord, help me to reach out to others and move toward Your marvelous Light in absolute trust.
                                                  —Marion Bond West

*Everlasting joy [shall be] upon their heads: they shall obtain
joy and gladness. . . .*   —Isaiah 35:10

❧ **O**ne day when my daughter Maria and I were playing on the bed, she suddenly pointed to the fine lines
beside my eyes.

"What are these?" she asked.

"Wrinkles," I said, thinking, *Oh, great, now my two-year-old
has to remind me that I'm not getting any younger.*

"Twinkles," she said, pleased with herself.

"No, wrin–" I stopped in mid-correction. "You know,
that makes them sound like something good, Maria.
Twinkles they are."

That night as I looked in the mirror, I realized that my
twinkles do come from smiling and laughing, forming a
kind of road map of the great joy with which God has
blessed my life. From parents who filled our house with
laughter and taught us not to take ourselves too seriously,
and brothers who are still two of the funniest people I
know, I learned the value of a laugh a day. If there's one
gift God has given me in abundance, it's joy, and I have
the twinkles to prove it.

I'm turning 40 in December, and while I haven't been
particularly excited about it, or about those subtle lines, or
my one pesky gray hair that returns each time I snip it off,
I'm ready to look at it all in a new way. Mark Twain wrote,
"Wrinkles should merely indicate where smiles have
been."

So, rejoice in the twinkles. They're a sign to the world
that God has given me a lot to smile and laugh about.

*Joyful Creator, in Your grace continue to fill my life with
laughter, joy, and an abundance of twinkles.*
                                        —Gina Bridgman

Thou shalt love thy neighbor as thyself. —Matthew 19:19

When my granddaughter Katie started school, she said to her mother the night before, "I'm shy. I don't know how to make friends."

Her mother replied, "You say, 'Hi. My name is Katie. Want to be friends?'" Katie nodded and practiced the words over and over before a full-length mirror.

The next day Katie came home smiling. "Guess what, Mom? I have two best friends. Katie and Libbie."

When Katie's mother visited the school that first week and looked at the list of children in the class, she found only Libbie's name. She asked her daughter, "Where's the other little girl named Katie?"

Katie answered, "*I'm* the other Katie! I counted myself as one of my best friends."

As my daughter related this story, I quietly remembered that I was 35 before I began to understand that self-love is the basis for relating to others. As a young mother, I found my four children, and especially my twins, were more than I could handle. I began to regard myself as a failure. One day, I just gave up and asked God to take over and meet all my needs. The first need He met was to give me a love for myself. It meant learning patience, accepting failure, finding a sense of humor, getting enough rest, asking for help. Motherhood taught me that loving myself *first* made me a better wife and mother to my family.

If you want to improve your relations with others, why not start practicing self-love today?

Continue to teach me, Father, how to be loving toward myself,
so that I might love others. —Marion Bond West

*Bring them [your children] up in the nurture and admonition of
the Lord.*   *—Ephesians 6:4*

🎀 The first thing I notice is the smell of crackling
bacon. I'm really here–vacation at my grandparents' cabin.
The sun gleams from the lake outside my bedroom window. Everything an eight-year-old boy could ask of a summer day. I make a break for the front door.

"Brock! It's devotion time."

Oh no. She caught me. I feel like the fish I had hoped to
hook. Bebe, my grandmother, reels me in. There she is
with sister Keri and my cousins Kristi, and Michel. *Girls.*
How can they act so content, sitting there waiting for my
grandmother to read from her daily devotion book?

Looking back I have to laugh. I am amazed at my grandmother's patience, trying to instill some good in the little
firecracker I was then.

"Brock, the Lord is your Shepherd (Psalm 23:1). Don't
forget that, son."

"Oh, Bebe, I'd rather go swimming."

And another time, "'Ask, and it shall be given you, Brock
(Matthew 7:7). The good Lord hears your prayers."

"Yes, Bebe. Isn't this a perfect day for hiking?" Yet over
the years those Bible verses have come to mean a lot to me.

I found an extra $40 in my pay. It was tempting, but I
knew it was a mistake. "A good name is rather to be chosen
than great riches" (Proverbs 22:1), Bebe said. Her words
won the day. I smiled to myself as I gave the money back.

"Harrison David Brockwell Kidd," I can hear Bebe say,
"the Lord loves you."

*Thank you for the Sunday school teachers, the church workers,
educators, moms, dads, and especially grandparents who never
give up on us.*   *—Brock Kidd*

21

Therefore, my beloved brethren, be ye steadfast, unmovable, always abounding in the work of the Lord, forasmuch as ye know that your labor is not in vain in the Lord.
—I Corinthians 15:58

The Centennial Celebration was to be the biggest gathering my childhood church had ever had, with four full days of activities. I planned to travel back from the West Coast to New York to attend, and for weeks I daydreamed about what the Evening of Remembrance might include. Perhaps the "Flying Evangelist" who took us on plane rides? Or the many talented musical groups who had come to share their faith? Maybe the dramatic candlelight New Year's Eve service we once had?

But I was in for a surprise. The cozy, hushed auditorium sheltered many precious faces. Some had white hair. Others who were once toddlers looked down at me. And as each one stood, they named individuals. Ida, the quiet, nursery teacher whom no one could remember *not* being there. They remembered the untiringly serving Pearl. Several people mentioned Betty's quiet faithfulness as a Sunday school teacher. "Betty's always there, always the same," one woman said with teariness. "That's meant a lot to me."

Nothing was said that evening about stupendous events or "big names." It dawned on me how very much we crave dependability and quiet steadfastness. These were the treasures to remember, the goals to try for.

I left that evening with a new perspective, and with a proud hand on Betty's freckled arm. You see, Betty's my mom.

Dear Lord, have I been pursuing "Christian showiness," hoping to win more favor and unforgettableness? Help me choose the better thing.
—Kathie Kania

22

Harken unto this . . . stand still, and consider the wondrous works of God.
                                                                    —Job 37:14

🍃 **M**y mother had few material things in her life, but cared for what she did have lovingly. With ten children in the house, sometimes some of her little treasures got broken. I can see her still, patiently trying to glue them back together.

"Why don't you just throw it in the trash, Mama?" I would ask.

"But you'll hardly be able to tell it's been broken when I finish with it," she would reply.

As for myself, I wanted nothing broken or ruined. When something bad happened to anything of mine, it went straight into the trash can. I demanded this kind of perfection for many years.

Then, seven years ago, I had a serious stroke and was left with several side effects, among them the inability to write or type. Doctors told me that I probably would never be able to do either again, and I was crushed. But I have since proven them wrong, and now can do both. Not perfectly, of course, as I once did, but I thank God every day for each imperfect page I am able to turn out, and I consider them miracles.

Today I find much value and beauty in things that are imperfect. For example, the very elderly neighbor who is right now approaching my door walks slowly and painfully with a metal walker. But her mind is so keen and her conversation so brilliant and interesting that a visit from her is always a joy. Incidentally, her walker is exactly like the one that was delivered to me a few days ago.

Oh, God, help me to ever see the value that often lies in imperfection.
                                                                    —Dorothy Nicholas

He that dwelleth in love dwelleth in God, and God in him.
—I John 4:16

❧ When my granddaughter Jennifer was 11, she met her Greatuncle Earl for the first time at a family reunion. Jennifer didn't know that Earl was a victim of Alzheimer's disease. My sister Alice had seated him in a comfortable chair near the kitchen doorway. I had greeted Earl and then backed away because he couldn't talk with me.

Jennifer, however, pulled up a chair close to him and began to tell him about her spring vacation. Earl didn't respond or even look at her, but she kept talking, her voice rising and falling as expressively as if he were answering. Finally, Earl turned his face toward her, and for a moment his eyes looked as if he might smile. He didn't. Jennifer continued as if he had, and from then on he kept his eyes fixed on her face. She talked to him for a long time before she excused herself and went out to play.

That scene stayed with me, and after Jennifer had gone, I remembered Elizabeth Barrett Browning's lines:

Earth's crammed with heaven,
And ever common bush afire with God.

It seemed that God had ignited a branch on our family tree and that Jennifer's innocent compassion had brought us a little bit of Heaven. Jennifer changed forever the way I treat people—not only those who cannot respond to me because disabilities, but also those who choose to ignore me or those whom I would like to ignore because I don't understand them. The gifts of love and attention work wonders.

Wherever I go, Lord, please let me be a spark for Your heavenly fire and transforming love. —Elsie Larson

LAUGHTER LINES

A sense of humor might be the most sensible thing we have … at least it seems that way sometimes. Just when we're in danger of taking ourselves too seriously or forgetting to enjoy life, we see the humor in the situation. Whether it's falling in the bathtub or learning to love our imperfections—a smile, a giggle or an all-out belly laugh is a great occurrence.

When you read the selections in this section, you'll recognize yourself in some of them, and find out we're not alone in our mistakes or in our ability to share a laugh.

A merry heart doeth good like a medicine.

—Proverbs 17:22

A TO Z

Thank You, God
for apples and almonds,
babies and banana cream pie,
chocolate chip cookies and checker games,
dogs and dominoes,
emerald green oceans and eggs over-easy,
faithful friends and fragrant forests,
giddy grandchildren and gracious gifts,
helping hands and heating pads,
ice cream cones and interesting issues.
For jellies and jams,
kites and kindred spirits,
lace and lavender,
memories and marshmallows,
nice neighbors and new beginnings,
old friends and Oreos,
peppermints and pumpkin pie,
quiet moments and questions answered,
roses and remedies.
For spaghetti and sensational songs,
tea and toast,
umbrellas and unicorns,
visions and violins,
walks and warm wool,
X-rays and xylophones,
yarns and yams,
zoos and a zest for living!

—Doris R. Mapes

I was baby-sitting three of my grandchildren, and it was time to bathe two-year-old Thomas. I got him and all his toys into the tub, and began to wash him, sitting at an angle on the edge so I could continue talking with Jamie and Katie, his sisters. Then, before I could catch myself, I lost my balance, slipped backward, and fell into the tub–fully clothed.

My granddaughters laughed hysterically. Thomas, observing them for a few seconds, threw his head back and joined in the laughter. As I sat in the warm water with my arms and legs extended, I felt this tremendous laugh making its way out. I leaned against the pink tiles and let it come. The four of us were joined together by our laughter, which lasted for perhaps three minutes and was exhausting and satisfying and unforgettable.

Of course, I wouldn't have laughed in my young motherhood days. I would have resented anything that made me look less than perfect, and would have been in a nasty mood for the rest of the evening, probably not speaking. And we would never have mentioned the incident again.

I'm glad I have finally learned–through experience, age, and God's grace–that there's a time to laugh, even at myself and my humanness.

Father, help me to see the lighter side of things.

—*Marion Bond West*

To him that is joined to all the living there is hope. . . .
—Ecclesiastes 9:4

For a couple of dogs living in New York City, Sally Brown, our cocker spaniel, and Marty, our yellow Lab, are pretty well mannered. But they can be a handful.

Taking advantage of the weather one Saturday, my wife Julee, Sally, Marty and I piled in a cab and headed up to Central Park. We were stalled in traffic when a horse pulling a carriage full of tourists stepped up and inclined its head to the rear window of our cab. Marty came unstrung, thrashing around the backseat. The terrified cabbie threw us out. I apologized and gave him a generous tip. He was smiling as we left him.

In the park, Sally snatched a hot dog out of a little girl's hand. I bought the little girl another hot dog while Julee apologized to the mother. The little girl gleefully fed her second hot dog to Marty. "She's always been afraid of dogs!" the mother said, laughing.

We then took the dogs to the lake. That went fine until a wedding party, resplendent in white, came down the path. Naturally, Sally and Marty emerged from the murky waters to investigate the new arrivals and, they had to shake out their sopping coats, splattering the bride and her maids with tiny drops of mud. Out of the corner of my eye, I saw Julee's lips moving in panicky prayer. All was well, though, and Marty and Sally ended up getting their picture taken with the bespattered bride.

A smiling cabbie, a slightly braver little girl, and an unusual wedding photograph—not such a bad afternoon at that. Maybe God was teaching us, slyly using our two gregarious pets, to hone our skills as humans.

I am grateful, Lord, when You reach into my day and train me to handle life's stickier situations.   *—Edward Grinnan*

Who through faith . . . out of weakness were made strong. . . .
                                            —Hebrews 11:33-34

🐌 I was in my early teens before I knew about one of my imperfections. I'd just appeared in a school play and believed I'd done pretty well. That included one woman who told my mother authoritatively that I showed great potential as an actor, but, something would have to be done about "his lisp."

There are things I'd never thought about: (1) becoming an actor and (2) my having a lisp. Nobody had mentioned it to me before. But from then on I was always aware of it. I tried to make fun of it, taking derisive pleasure in telling friends, "I lithp exthept when I thay Ithaca," or laboring for hours on making a translation of the Gettysburg Address without the letter s (don't try it). In our daily chapel at school, I'd often ask God to do something about it. The best He seemed to do was to have people tell me they hardly noticed it.

God did do something. Some years ago, forced to make a speech, I began my talk with an attempt to disarm my listeners by saying, "the terrible thing about a lisp is you can't *say* it without *doing* it." Later, a man came up to me and said, "You haven't accepted that lisp of yours, have you?"

I was so surprised that I could only nod. "A wise man once told me," he went on, "that if you accept your limitations, you go beyond them. Think about it."

Think about it I did.

So today, if there's anybody reading this who'd like me to come and speak, I'm available. But fair warning: You, too, will have to accept my limitations.

*Forgive me for bothering You about that speech problem, Lord.
It seemed important at the time.*   —Van Varner

This is my commandment, That ye love one another, as I have loved you.   —John 15:12

Abraham Lincoln had a unique way of saying things. He could use words to make people think about issues, like slavery and states rights. But he could use words to make people laugh, too. One day a man came to Lincoln and asked, "How long should a man's legs be?"

Lincoln looked first at the short man's little legs, then down at his own long ones. Slowly, he smiled. "Well," he said, "I reckon a man's legs out to be long enough to reach the floor."

And that's the way God made each of us: with legs just the right length to reach the floor. And ears big enough to hear the song of birds and the laughter of children. With mouths wide enough for smiles and arms perfectly formed for hugs. Shoulders perfect for leaning on, backs meant to be patted. We've each got just the right equipment to help make the world a better place.

Creator of all perfect things, thank You for the opportunity to serve my fellow human beings.   —Mary Lou Carney

We are fools for Christ's sake. . . . —I Corinthians 4:10

It's Sunday morning and I'm sitting on an old tub in the furnace room of our church, wearing an orange and purple clown suit. I am to make a surprise appearance in the sanctuary to promote Vacation Bible School. This is my very first time at clowning, and I am struggling with stage fright. My bifocals are steaming up, the ends of my yarn wig are scratching my neck, and perspiration is dampening my striped socks and polka-dotted shoes.

But what's worse is the niggling question about propriety: Will a middle-aged deacon's wife who dares to breach long-established ideas of decorum in our conservative church alienate the very people she hopes to reach?

Filtering down through the air duct comes the hymn, "Take Time to Be Holy." I cannot expect certain church members to equate a ridiculous clown with holiness.

But wait! There are words in that hymn that I have never really heard before: "Make friends of God's children." Isn't that what I intend to do by pantomiming in my colorful costume while the minister introduces me as Rosco, the Vacation Bible School mascot? Saying a quick prayer, adjust my huge bow tie, and waddle up the stairs.

For a moment the congregation is silent. Then, one by one, wide-eyed children begin to giggle and somber adults cannot suppress amused grins. At the suggestion that perhaps nobody has time for Vacation Bible School, Rosco cries with disappointment. "So who will come and make Rosco happy?" asks the minister. Everybody in the congregation raises a hand, and Rosco exits merrily, stage right.

Father, give me the courage to use new and creative ways to attract people to You.
                                          —Alma Barkman

His divine power hath given unto us all things that pertain unto life and godliness through the knowledge of him that hath called us to glory and virtue. —2 Peter 1:3

❧ I'm on another diet. This one claims, "Never feel hungry." If that's the case, then why was it so hard for me to clean up the kitchen today? Why did I have to squeeze my eyes shut to put away the peanut butter and mash the macaroni leftovers into the dog food so I wouldn't gobble them up?

My grandmother would have sized up the situation using her own quaint terminology: "The trouble with you is that you're *mouth-hungry*, not *stomach-hungry*." And she'd be right. My stomach was not grumbling, nor did it have pangs. All I really wanted was to indulge in a great feast of flavors, textures, and aromas.

I have been *mouth-hungry* in other ways, too. When my typewriter broke, my husband suggested we buy a slightly better one that would do more things and still be within our budget. I wanted a word processor with features even a publishing house wouldn't need. *Mouth-hungry*. And when we bought a used pickup truck, the man said, "You can keep the fancy 'mag' wheels for $200 more."

"Sure," I said.

"No," my husband said.

Mouth-hungry. Going way beyond the need. Maybe I should take a better look at being content with what is obviously enough. I may lose a little weight along the way, too!

Lord, Grandma was putting it kindly calling me mouth-hungry—it's really greed. Help me to put Your kingdom first, and to be thankful for the many things I do have. —Kathie Kania

Their faces were not ashamed. —Psalm 34:5

I never have been known for my athletic ability. (In fact, I was once asked to leave a bowling team because I lowered their average so much.) So when I saw the sign for a golf-putting contest to benefit a charity, I hurried right by.

But unbeknownst to me, my husband Paul paid the $2, one for him and one for me. We each got a chance to hit the ball down a long green strip of Astroturf. (The contest organizers were trying to beat the distance in the *Guinness Book of World Records*.)

The first swing I took missed the ball completely. The emcee kindly gave me a second chance, and I clipped the corner of the ball and watched it dribble inches down the green.

My face flamed as the emcee announced to the huge crowd, "Say, she's got a real shot at winning the booby prize!" I yanked Paul's arm, and we scurried away, but not before I heard the emcee boom out my name: "Linda was our most valuable player! You know, if Arnold Palmer was up here, *nobody* would have the courage to go next. But after someone like Linda, people say, 'Boy, if *she* was willing to get up there and putt . . . ' and we get more dollars for charity!"

For the first time in my life, I was able to laugh at my own ineptitude! Maybe sometimes it's just as helpful to be the worst as to be the best.

God, help me always to remember: I don't have to be the best in order to be valuable—to other people or to You.

—Linda Neukrug

Take not the word of truth utterly out of my mouth. . . .
—Psalm 119:43

🍂 The lemon pie I'd brought for dinner was very well received. And no wonder! The crust was made by Pillsbury and the filling with help from Betty Crocker. I guess you could say I'd "assembled" the pie rather than baked it. At dessert time the guests buzzed, "Linda, this pie is absolutely delicious! Did you make it from scratch?" But instead of saying, "No," I told myself I couldn't answer right away because I had a forkful of lemon pie in my mouth. Finally, I said with a smile, "Well, I didn't grow the lemons. . . ." Then I soaked up the praise.

To me it was just a little fib. So I was surprised at my husband Paul's reaction. As soon as we were out the door he asked, "Why didn't you tell them the truth?" I could tell from the puzzled look on his face that he was honestly curious. So I considered the question, *Why hadn't I.*

The answer was simple. I felt ashamed that I wasn't a better cook. I wanted to do everything perfectly. But once I'd brought my reason into the light, I saw how foolish it was! After all, I didn't choose my friends for their cooking skills, but for other reasons, like their compassion, loyalty, sense of fun—and yes, their honesty. Even about the little things in life—like lemon pies!

Which is why, the very next day, I showed up on my friend's porch. "Would you like my recipe for last night's lemon pie?" I asked with a grin. She looked surprised and nodded, and I thrust a paper sack into her hands. In it? A box of Pillsbury pie crust and some instant lemon pudding.

Thank You, God, for reminding me that I don't have to be perfect to be loved by others—or by You.   *—Linda Neukrug*

O Lord, be not far from me. —Psalm 35:22

My husband David and I have just worked out at our neighborhood YMCA, and I am waiting for him. I have not less than a *jillion* things to do before the day is over, and the thought of the long day ahead fills my insides with a familiar panic. I pace up and down the hall, I find myself staring at a sign posted on the wall. *You are here*, it says. A red arrow points to a certain location marked with an X on the building's blueprint.

I am still standing there looking at the sign when David comes. "This is crazy," I say to him, "but I feel so reassured knowing exactly where I am in this busy day."

Later, I am working at my computer when the buzzer on the dryer sounds. On my way to remove David's shirts, I smell the chicken dish cooking in the kitchen and change my direction to check on it. Passing the dining room, I notice that I haven't yet set the table for tonight's guests. A moment of cold fear falls over me. *Can I really handle all of this?* Then I remember the sign. "You are here," I remind myself as I open the oven door. The casserole is fine.

After I have the shirts on hangers, I return to my desk and jot down all the things I need to accomplish, numbering them by priority. "You are here," I say out loud as I draw a red arrow to number one on the blueprint of my day.

Realizing that today actually can be managed, one task at a time, I stop and smile. "I am here," I say to God, "and You are here. Let's turn this into a good, productive day together." And we do!

Dear Father, my days are so full and I find myself over-whelmed. Give me the peace that comes from knowing that where I am, You are, and together we can handle whatever comes.
—Pam Kidd

Judge not according to the appearance. . . .   —John 7:24

I was sure that the young fellow sitting across from me at the airport, as we waited to board our plane to Minneapolis, was a foreigner. Without a word being said, one clue announced, "I am a stranger to Western ways." The giveaway was a satin brand-name label that remained sewn to the outside sleeve of his new gray suit coat.

Perhaps someone had said to him, "Clip off that label," but he misunderstood. Or perhaps he simply thought that leaving the label intact was the thing to do. Either way, the label unknowingly revealed something about the boy.

Three hours in-flight gave me time to consider the labels I leave on myself and others: too-old-to-change, short-fused, crowd-pleaser. . . . I thought about Zacchaeus, notorious as "the chief tax collector." But Jesus already knew that label was incomplete. There was more to Zacchaeus, a man ready to be redeemed, so the Lord called out, Zacchaeus, . . . today I must abide at thy house (Luke 19:5).

It seems that the problem with labels is not that they tell us too much about another person, but that they tell us too little! By the time we landed, I'd made a resolution. I could start clipping away at the labels that limit my compassion. Mike is "the life of the party," but he undoubtedly has a serious side. *Clip, clip.* Susan is "materialistic," but I'll bet she'd love a simple poem for her birthday. *Clip, clip.*

Can you think of labels you have put on yourself or others that might be prayerfully, gently, permanently removed?

Dear Lord, help me to overcome the limiting labels I assign to others and help me, instead, to know them more fully.
—Stephanie Lindsell

God hath chosen the foolish things of the world to confound the wise. . . . —*I Corinthians* 1:27

⮑ One afternoon I wandered into the arts and crafts room at a conference. I scooped up a handful of clay, put it on the pottery wheel, and began to spin a pot. When I finished, I had produced the most pathetically lopsided pot. As I looked at it in disgust, the resident potter appeared. "I think I should just toss this thing in the trash," I said.

"I know how you feel. The first pot I ever made looked just like that and I hated it," she said. "But I decided to save it. In fact, it sits in a prominent place in my house."

She explained. "You see, I used to be a real perfectionist. I rejected whatever I did that didn't meet my own rigid standards. My lopsided pot reminded me that it's okay not to be perfect, that it's even desirable."

"Well, think about it," she said. "If you're perfect, you won't have anyone like yourself to relate to. It would be awfully lonely being perfect, don't you think?"

I thought about my own imperfections, and how I berated myself for them. My house wasn't spotless. And seven times out of ten I burned whatever I put in the toaster. Sometimes it took me three months to answer a letter. I'd gained a few pounds and broken promises to myself to take them off. I fussed at my family when they didn't deserve it . . . *lopsided pots*, all of them!

It is important to try for excellence and improve, but it is also important to accept myself in spite of my imperfections, to relax my standards and join the human race. I took that silly pot home and put it in my study. And funny thing—whenever people come to visit, they gravitate to that pot right away. Something in them understands.

You know what an imperfect pot I can be, God. Thanks for loving me anyway. —*Sue Monk Kidd*

*He that covereth his sins shall not prosper; but whoso confesseth
and forsaketh them shall have mercy.* —Proverbs 28:13

🍂 Mistakes. I seem to make lots of them. I call someone by the wrong name. I say something when I should
say nothing, or nothing when I should say something. I
throw a red sock with the white laundry or forget to turn
off the horses' water so it runs down the hill for hours.
Usually, when I realize my mistake, I get all mad at myself
and start carrying around a grudge—*against me.*

But a friend recently told me a story about mistakes that
changed my response. Her father visited a Persian rug
factory where exquisite, one-of-a-kind rugs are handwo-
ven. He asked what happened when the weavers made a
mistake. "Do they have to go back and start over again?"
he questioned.

"Oh, no," came the answer. "They call in the master
weaver who weaves the mistake right into the pattern."

The very next time I made a mistake, I tried the Persian
rug formula. After writing two important letters, I dropped
them in the corner mailbox and then discovered I'd sealed
them in the wrong envelopes. Instead of standing there
and scolding myself, I mentally raised my hand to the
Master Weaver. "I goofed, God, and this could be embar-
rassing. Please weave the mistake into something good."

Two days later, the telephone rang. "I just got your
friend's letter in my envelope," a merry voice said. "You
don't know how much I needed a reminder today that
everyone makes mistakes. Thanks."

*Into Your hands, Master Weaver, I commit my mistakes—big
ones and little ones.* —Carol Kuykendall

Then was our mouth filled with laughter. . . .   —Psalm 126:2

❧ I was tired. It was the end of a long school day at the end of June, and teaching was getting me down. The kids were eager to begin summer vacation, and while I understood, it was my job to settle them down. I assigned a composition. The topic, I announced, drawing one from thin air, was "My Pet Peeve." Frankly, any topic would have done. I was merely trying to gain a little peace and quiet. "My pet peeve," I commented in a serious tone, "is students who don't take their work seriously." I looked pointedly at Cliff, the class "wise guy." Oh, he was genuinely funny and not malicious, but I felt that the classroom was not the place for any hijinks or jokes. "Remember, report card time is coming . . . *blah . . . blah . . . blah. . . .*" I droned on, boring even myself.

Of course, that night I had to pay for it by marking 35 papers. I groaned, even more so when I discovered Cliff's essay on top. My forehead creased as I read his first line. Then I burst out laughing. "My pet, Peeve," he had written, " is a good pet. He has to be fed and watered three times a day. He likes to be walked at a brisk pace. . . ."

Laughing, I shoved the remainder of the papers back into my briefcase and the next day announced, "As a 'Here Comes Summer' gift, everyone gets an A on that paper!" Then I silently thanked Cliff for teaching *me* an important lesson: *Lighten up!*

God, help me to stop taking my life, and myself, oh-so-seriously all the time! And if there are people in my life with a sense of humor, may I learn from them!   —Linda Neukrug

This is the day which the Lord hath made; we will rejoice and be glad in it. —Psalm 118:24

When we were youngsters growing up in our sleepy Southern town of Savannah, most of the grandparents and parents of my friends seemed rather staid and sober folk, not very exciting. But there was one memorable exception: Miss Lucy. Miss Lucy was a widow lady in her 60s, or thereabouts, who lived with her sister Clara. Clara was prim and proper, but Miss Lucy was a live wire, full of charm and sparkle and enthusiasm and energy.

One day, in the course of assuring some of us that age need not be a barrier to anything, Miss Lucy asserted that she could still stand on her head whenever she felt like it. When we looked doubtful, she proceeded to do so, clamping her skirt between her knees and beaming at us upside down.

"Oh, Lucy," said Clara disapprovingly. "Do be your age!"

Miss Lucy righted herself and looked at her sister. "Be your age?" she said. "What sort of nonsense is that? How can anyone be anything *but* their age? The trick is to *love* your age, whatever it is. Love it when you're young and strong and foolish. Love it when you're old and wise. Love it in the middle when the challenges come and you can fly at them and solve some of them, maybe most of them. If you love your age, you'll never go around wishing you were some other age. Think about that now and then, Clara. Might do you good!"

I don't know whether Miss Lucy's words had any effect on her sister. I do know they did on me. They were spoken more than 50 years ago, but, you see, I remember them still.

Lord, teach us to love all the years of life You've given us.
—Arthur Gordon

Ye thought evil against me, but God meant it unto good. . . .
—Genesis 50:20

🍃 I have a friend who is 50 years older than I. Her name is Gladys and I adore her. People ask me what in the world I get out of a friendship separated by half a century. They assume I've befriended Gladys because she's old and needy, and I'm just trying to do a good deed. But believe me, that's not it. If anything, it's the other way around: I'm the one in need of her.

Let me tell you why. One day Gladys started to tell me a story, then stopped and rubbed her forehead. "I can't remember how it goes," she said. "My memory isn't what it used to be. But that's not all bad." She chuckled and pointed to a piece of paper on her refrigerator with some words written by Montaigne.

Advantages of a Bad Memory
1. One cannot be a good liar.
2. One cannot tell long stories.
3. One forgets offenses.
4. One enjoys places and books a second time around.

That's why I adore Gladys, and why I need her more than she needs me. Because through her wise, witty, and upbeat attitude, she teaches me to take life's inevitable setbacks and find the advantages in them. She takes on both the good and bad in life without becoming embittered or despairing. She may have a bad memory, but I still look at her and think, *She's what I want to be when I grow up.*

Help me, God, to look at life's disadvantages through the "eyes of Gladys."
—Sue Monk Kidd

The hoary head is a crown of glory, if it be found in the way
of righteousness.   —Proverbs 16:31

☙ In my family it happens at age 42. Reading glasses.
When my dad turned 42, he got them. Two years later, at
age 42, my mom got them. And a couple of years ago,
when I turned 42, I was no different.

Before I turned 43, I noticed my knees started cracking
every time I walked upstairs. Then my left shoulder ached
whenever the humidity rose. Not long after that, my son
Andrew announced, "You sure do have a lot of gray hairs
on top, Mom."

My mother said it best when she recited her favorite
poem shortly after she got her first pair of reading glasses.

I can see through my bifocals,
My dentures fit me fine.
My hearing aid does wonders,
But Lord, I miss my mind!

I laughed with her when she recited it years ago, and
now that I'm reaching middle age myself, I've decided to
keep my mother's sense of humor about it. I've also added
this to my favorite quotations about aging: "Age is a matter of mind. If you don't mind, it doesn't matter."

Lord, whether I'm 32, 42, or 92, remind me to look for the
positives and not dwell on the "reading glasses" of life!
                                        —Patricia Lorenz

AS GOD MADE ME

Do you wish you were smarter, taller, thinner? We all have those wishes—sometimes several times a day. The fact is we are perfect creations of God our Father. We are all part of God's plan and He loves us exactly the way He made us. Why would we want to change that?

When you read about the little boy who knows he is a gift and the woman who learns it is more important to sing than to sing perfectly, you'll see how each of us is part of God's plan. God can use our imperfections to reach out to people or to help us grow—they're not imperfections to him, they're part of His perfect plan.

God commendeth his love toward us.

—ROMANS 5:8

GLAD TO BE ME

Oh, God, you've made so many things;
The fish that swims, the bird that sings,
The world so big, the ant so small—
How wisely you have made them all!
You formed the ocean, large and wide
Where countless creatures live and hide,
And mountains high where eagles rest,
And tree on plain for robin's nest.
The flowers bloom so beautifully
That I must stop to smell, touch, see.
All people You have caused to be—
I'm so glad, God, that You made me.

—Eileen M. Berger

Blessed are all they that put their trust in [the Lord].

&❧ **O**nce, I visited the shop of a violin maker. The man patiently explained the art of violin making to me, demonstrating the use of his wood-shaping tools.

"I suppose the wood used in your instrument is the most important element," I suggested, pointing to some pieces of maple and spruce that he had imported from the highlands of Germany.

"It is imperative that you use high quality, seasoned wood to achieve resonance," he agreed. "But there is something more important to the finished product: the musician who plays it. In the hands of a master, even a flawed instrument can produce beautiful music."

I've thought of his words many times since. What is true of violins is also true of people. I met a young man who had lost the use of his legs. He had been an outstanding athlete, but now is reduced to watching sports. I say "reduced" but this is a misnomer. He is as full of life and as involved in life as anyone I've ever met, active as a church officer, baseball coach, and community leader.

"I can do all things through Christ which strenghtheneth me," he testifies joyfully (Philippians 4:13). His body may not be perfect, but his spirit compensates for it. And because he has put himself in the hands of the Master, his life produces beautiful music.

God can do the same for you and me, no matter what our shortcomings, no matter what our flaws.

Teach us, God, to . .
Live life without complaint,
To hug what is, not what ain't.

He calleth his own sheep by name. . . . —John 10:3

🐝 I found a gift in a grocery sack today. I was putting away the food I'd brought in from the car, checking the items against the cash register receipt. Skim milk, orange juice, Earl Grey tea, carrots. . . . How could three bags of groceries come to $62.07?

That's when I came to my gift—on that white strip of figures from the register. At the bottom of the long column, just below the dismaying total, I read: "Valued Customer 43220884464."

I gaped at the 11-digit figure. Was I really valued customer forty-three billion, two hundred twenty million, eight hundred eighty-four thousand, four hundred sixty-four? Truly valued, as the receipt claimed, among so many?

It's a question I remember asking, many years ago, of God. In a universe with billions of galaxies, on a planet with billions of people, could He possibly care about me?

Staring at the register receipt, I recalled His answer. *I do not count My children*, He seemed to say, *I name them*. It was a new thought to me—the importance of names, all through the Bible. How genuinely valued a name makes us! To my heavenly Father I am not a number, but an individual. Not Valued Child 873972491, but Elizabeth. Known by name, called by name, written by His own hand in the Book of Life.

I'm so grateful, Father, that You count not in billions, but one by one. —Elizabeth Sherrill

Train up a child in the way he should go: and when he is old, he will not depart from it. —*Proverbs* 22:6

🦋 **M**y father and mother were domestics who cooked. They worked from dawn to dusk, often seven days a week. During house parties their workday stretched into morning hours without additional pay. When dishes and pots overflowed their employers' sinks, I was expected to help.

Father and Mother never complained. Their conversation echoed with admiration for their employers. I was ashamed and I felt their employers took advantage of Father and Mother. Why didn't they speak up for their rights?

I vowed to escape, but how? The answer: Get an education! So with scholarships, long hours in the college kitchen, and sacrifices at home, I completed college. From there it was into teaching and on to industry. I seized the opportunity and moved from the machine shop to engineering technician to senior technical writer. Education paid off and, secretly, I felt I had done it on my own.

Then, one day, my supervisor paused at my desk and said, "I would love to have met your parents. They taught you well. You are a worker and a gentleman!"

It wasn't my academic training alone. Father and Mother had received little appreciation, yet their devotion had gained them the reputation for being skillful, industrious, honest, and diligent. They had instilled this in me. What a precious gift!

There is more. After retirement, I returned to cooking, washing, ironing, and caring for the lawn. I acquired a secret: It isn't the job or the title. It's completing the task and doing it well. Father and Mother were experts. They were the reasons for my success.

Dear Father, please remove the pride that blinds and binds me. Free me to follow Your will. —*Oscar Greene*

So we, being many, are one body in Christ. . . . Having then gifts differing according to the grace that is given to us. . . .
—Romans 12:5-6

☙ Last Sunday, the choir director came up to my daughter Karen who, like her mother, doesn't carry a tune very well. "I've noticed that you don't sing the hymns," he told her.

"I can't sing!" she said.

"It doesn't matter," he replied. "Really! Some voices are right on pitch, and we need those people. But in the congregation, we also need the voices that aren't perfectly pitched in order to round out the sound. All of them blend together *and God hears it whole!* So please, go ahead and sing!" Karen decided to do just that next Sunday . . . and her mom might even get up the courage to do it, too.

Maybe it's the same with any other ability. The world surely needs the very talented ones, those who truly excel. But perhaps, just as in the singing of hymns, those with average talent still have a contribution to make. So, with my writing and teaching, I will quit comparing myself to others. Instead, I'll work hard at what I do. I'll sing my own part of the song, knowing that "God hears it whole!"

Thank You, Lord, for giving each of us valued parts in Your inclusive song. —Marilyn Morgan Helleberg

For he that is mighty hath done to me great things. . . .
—Luke 1:49

🐟 Jenny is an unprepossessing child. Shy, awkward, a little ungainly, she seemed an unlikely choice for Mary in the church Christmas pageant. No parent was heard to complain, but then our pageant has always had its casting irregularities

That morning, there was the usual display of nerves and high spirits, the last-minute tweaking of a halo, the mouthing of a well-rehearsed line. The Annunciation came early. A teenaged boy wearing sneakers underneath his white robe told Mary that she would bear the Baby Jesus. Jenny, dressed in blue, walked down the center aisle and responded, "My soul doth magnify the Lord, and my spirit hath rejoiced in God my Savior" (Luke 1:46-47).

Jenny's voice was strong and confident, filling the church. Her diction was crystal clear. To my amazement and to everyone else's, she went on, "For he hath regarded the low estate of his handmaiden. . . ." She was going to recite all ten verses of Luke's song of Mary (1:46-55). We sat on the edge of our pews. Before our eyes, Jenny was transformed from a nine-year-old wallflower to a brave, commanding soul.

Never missing a beat, she made her way through the entire speech. The congregation burst into spontaneous applause. Better than any preacher, Jenny had given us the message of that moment. God could take a young peasant girl and make her the mother of His Son. God could transform a life into something awe-inspiring.

Take my life, Lord, and let it be changed by You.
—Rick Hamlin

O Lord. . . . I will praise thee, for I am fearfully and wonder-
fully made; marvelous are thy works. . . . —Psalm 139:1,14

One of the most cherished moments of our day
comes when, as a family, we join hands around the dinner
table and give thanks for all the blessings God has given
us. As the children were growing up, this became a choice
opportunity for them to learn how to pray out loud, develop
the gift of a grateful heart, and speak conversationally
with God.

One evening when shepherd's pie, the children's
favorite, was on the table, six-year-old Ian enthusiastically
volunteered to say the blessing. After he had duly thanked
God for the food and the highlights of the day, he
paused—and then added, "And thank You, God, for the
nice little boy You gave this family!"

"Nice little boy!" I gasped. "Where?"

"Right here," he grinned, pointing to himself. "I was
thanking God for me!"

Doing the dishes later that night, I thought, *The boy has
a point.* We all come tagged with the designer label:
"Individually Crafted with the Compliments of Your
Creator."

Suddenly, I was overwhelmed. Why, in all my years of
thanksgiving, I had never ever thanked God for me!
Hands dripping wet with suds, eyes spilling tears of wonder, there and then I quietly said, "Thank You, God, for all
the workmanship You put into making me!"

Take time today to thank Him for the designer
original—*you.*

*It is too wonderful for us, Lord, when we think that You have
numbered each hair and designed each cell of all that we are.
Thank You that You are constantly shaping each of us into
individual creations. Amen.* —Fay Angus

Then shall all the trees of the wood rejoice. —Psalm 96:12

"Raise your hands and shout hallelujah!" the song leader said, but I slid lower into my seat and felt my face turning pink. When it comes to praising God in public, I'm not very demonstrative. I admire those who can clap their hands and shout praise to God, but I'm so inhibited, I can't even lead a small group in silent prayer.

One summer afternoon I was taking my daily prayer walk in the country, and I sat down on a log by some white oak trees to rest. I felt a warm, sweet breeze ruffle my hair, then listened as it wove its way through the trees behind me like an invisible spirit.

When I opened my pocket Bible, I read a passage from Psalms that said, "Let the trees of the forest rustle with praise" (96:12). That text helped me to see that there are many good ways of praising God besides shouting or clapping. Leaves can't do anything but hang there on the limb or wiggle a little when a breath of wind disturbs them, but by their very nature they reflect the creative power and beauty of God.

On the way back to the car, I decided that I would try to be a little more demonstrative in worship, but that I would no longer berate myself for not being able to praise God in every fashion.

When I'm asked to shout but can only rustle, I'll remember that God knows that I am praising Him. It's my own very quiet nature–created in His image.

Lord, I know that You hear me, even when I don't shout.
—Daniel Schantz

And all that believed were together, and had all things common.
—Acts 2:44

❧ Some years ago, one of the young men in our neighborhood became a source of anxiety to his family and friends. Freddy dropped out of school, grew his hair long, dressed in an unkempt manner, and was running a mild war with his parents. I may have been the only person on our block who experienced no concern about his future. Here is the reason for my confidence.

When my son Ben was seven years old, he borrowed Freddy's bicycle. Freddy was eleven and just the week before had been given a brand-new ten-speed. This was an unlikely bike for him to have, for his parents were not wealthy enough to purchase things like that casually. He worshipped that bike and knew that if anything happened to it, he should not expect another one. Nevertheless, he lent it to my Benjamin.

That is why Ben was crying as he lay beside the spilled bike in our backyard. He had caught a crack with the front tire, and now he had to tell Freddy that he had bent and scratched the bike. I decided to soften the blow by finding Freddy and breaking the news.

He was around the corner. "Freddy," I said, "Ben crashed on your bike."

"Is he hurt?" Freddy asked. And that is all he asked.

From that moment to this, I have had no fears about what kind of man Freddy will become.

Lord, teach me to value people before things. *—John Cowan*

P.S. Freddy did not go to college. For a couple of years he washed dishes for pay. Now he is in a technical school learning about the electronics he loves.

Thy word is a lamp unto my feet, and a light unto my path.
—Psalm 119:105

🐝 Our community Adult Education program was offering a class in self-improvement. *Well,* I decided after giving thought to my haphazard and undisciplined ways, *I certainly can stand a bit of that.* And so I enrolled, hoping for some bit of modern-day magic, some simple method of self-programming, to help me shape up.

And you know what I read in my notebook after I came home from the first class? "For as he thinketh in his heart so is he" (Proverbs 23:7). "As ye sow, so shall ye reap" (Galatians 6:7). "Love thy neighbor as thyself" Matthew (19:19). All of this "new" miraculous advice I received was right there in my own Bible!

No wonder that Book, written so long ago, is still the world's bestseller. If I want to shape up, I don't need a fancy class or program—I can just open my Bible.

For self-improvement, God, I'll reach for The Book. It's as close as my bedside table. —Aletha Jane Lindstrom

[I] will be a Father unto you, and ye shall be my sons and daughters, saith the Lord Almighty. —II Corinthians 6:18

I was astonished to tears at the lifelike oil portrait my artist friend Eva Llanos did for the three-to-five year olds' Sunday school classroom. It was a copy of the famous one by Frances Hook, where Jesus is holding a child's face in both of His strong, carpenter's hands. The outstanding feature of this picture is the unconditional love burning in Jesus' eyes as He gazes into the face of this child.

I hung it over our altar where we gather for storytime and worship. But it wasn't just the children who were mesmerized. The adults, too, came to see. Early one Sunday, a woman I didn't know came in and stood for a long time not saying anything, just looking over the altar into the picture. Finally, I heard her whisper, "I wish my father would have looked at me like that."

I didn't answer. She wasn't talking to me. But a moment later her face lit up like the child's in the picture, and I knew God had slipped the truth into her heart: Her Father does look at her like that. And at you and me.

Lord Jesus, thank You for showing us the face of the Father in the face of Jesus. Help us, through faith, to accept His love.
—*Shari Smyth*

Let brotherly love continue.   —*Hebrews* 13:1

🌬 Every morning before work I like to sit in the clouds.
I mean, I sit in the men's steam room at my gym.

You hear amazing things: men's voices bragging or complaining about work, bragging or complaining about their
wives, bragging or complaining about their children.
There's something therapeutic about sitting in a room
where you can barely see your hand in front of your face,
like sitting in white darkness and sounding off about life.

Today there were just three of us. Perhaps because he
felt comfortably anonymous, the man on my left suddenly
said, "I haven't had a drink in over a week."

The man on my right volunteered, "I haven't had a drink
in five years."

"How do you do it?" the man on my left asked softly.
"It's the hardest thing I've ever tried. But I know if I keep
drinking I'm gonna' lose everything. I saw my dad go
through it, saw him lose it all. Still, I want to drink."

Then the man with five years of sobriety told an amazing story of how his life was nearly destroyed by alcohol.
He talked about his recovery, the faith that he had found,
and the life that he rebuilt. His voice flowed with gratitude. He asked the man on my left which way he was
going when he left the gym. "Uptown," the man replied.

"I'll walk with you. Maybe we'll grab a cup of coffee."

With that they were gone. Later, as I dressed, I wondered who they were. But I couldn't tell, and it didn't
matter. What did matter is that I had seen God working in
a most unusual place, as is so often the case.

You never know what you'll find in the clouds.

Make me ever vigilant, God, for signs of You at work.
                                        —*Edward Grinnan*

He that keepeth understanding shall find good.

—Proverbs 19:8

❧ Years ago, our son was completing his dental internship at an Ohio hospital and was seeking to purchase a practice in New England. He had shared these plans with my wife Ruby and me and had asked my opinion.

He would be the first professional of our race to settle in that town and I recalled the cold stares, the silent treatment, the isolation, and the remarks when I started my first job. Acceptance eventually came, but what if our son was rejected? What if the dental practice failed? What if our grandchild was isolated? Deeply troubled, I wrote to our son, suggesting he remain in Ohio.

Now I held in my hand the reply. "Dad, you have let us down. We feel disappointed to know you don't believe in us. We are praying, and we will trust in the Lord."

The neighbors welcomed them. One mowed their lawn as they unpacked. Others felled trees and stacked wood for the winter. Several alerted the family to the best places to shop. In time, the dental practice flourished. Ten years passed before we discussed the letter. There was pain, but without it, I never would have seen the truth about my own fears and the limits they put on me.

Taking risks, overcoming obstacles, and facing the unknown are challenges we're all called to accept at one time or another. Painful stares, distrust, and critical words may face you today, but they also clear the way for a better understanding of yourself and others. Carry the badge of faith and let God's goodness go with you to transform hearts and inspire others to better living.

Father, help me to move past my fears and the fears of others so that I may live freely to serve You. —Oscar Greene

God hath chosen the weak things of the world to confound the
things which are mighty. —*I Corinthians* 1:27

❧ You might think that a college teacher would feel
smart, but not this one. Every day of my 21-year career, I
have wrestled with deep feelings of inadequacy.

"It's God's way of keeping you humble," my wife Sharon
says.

"But I don't like this feeling."

"Now you know how your students feel. You can sym-
pathize. Besides, you would get lazy and careless if you
felt too confident. You would stop studying."

I shrug. "But people think college teachers know everything, and I don't. There's too much to know."

She wraps her arms around me and presses her nose to
mine. "Then people will just have to be disappointed."

My worry lines dissolve into a smile. "What's for
supper?"

"Don't ask. It's a flop. I can't cook anymore. I feel so
inadequate in the kitchen these days."

My turn. "It's God's way of keeping you humble!"

"Get out of here!"

You know, I think Sharon is right. Have you ever
thought to thank God for those feelings of inadequacy
that keep you trying harder?

Lord, I am week and needy. I'm trusting You to help me.
—*Daniel Schantz*

57

I will both lay me down in peace, and sleep. . . . —Psalm 4:8

❧ I can picture myself on *Oprah Winfrey* now. She looks at me somewhat sympathetically at first, then almost sneers. "Let me get this straight. You're 17, and you still enjoy being tucked in and saying night-time prayers with your mother?" Collective gasps begin to roil from the audience while younger members laugh. An eminent Austrian psychiatrist on the panel ventures, "I had a case very much like this in Vienna once. We cured her with shock therapy." Oprah pauses, reflects, then finally confesses that she had a similar problem as a young adult but cured herself with herbal teas and vitamin supplements.

What can I say? I'm an incurable "now-I-lay-me-down-to-sleeper" and "tuckaholic." Being comforted by Mom and saying my prayers with her is a traditional luxury I know won't last forever, so we enjoy it while we can. Sleep, I find, comes easily when you know you're being watched over and loved.

When I go away to school next fall, I'll miss having Mom near, but I'm sure that around our usual bedtime she'll find some excuse to putter in my room, straighten my desk, and absently plump my pillow. We'll be close in thought, and God will be there to "tuck me in" before I sleep.

Lord, let me find my place in the world with You always by my side.
          —Jenny Mutzbauer

When I am weak, then am I strong. —II Corinthians 12:10

Coatrooms. Milk breaks. The playground. Dusting erasers. Before closed-circuit TV, computer labs, and mentor programs, grammar school was a simple place where a portrait of George Washington hung beside the American flag and you could rely on spelling bees, reading groups, recess, music class, . . . and the rhythm band.

My destiny, I felt, was to play the triangle in the rhythm band. But the triangle seemed to belong to shiny girls with natural talent and natural curls. Always, I was handed a pair of smooth wooden sticks. Remember the *click-click-click* made by less-talented children as they banged those sticks together in the background? That was me. I dreamed of the day I would stand in the front row, triangle poised in midair . . . the star. But no matter how frantically I waved my hand, . . . "And Pamela," my teacher would say in an overly cheerful voice, "you may play the sticks today."

I learned a lot of things in school. Reading, writing, arithmetic, being nice to people, fighting for what's right. But the rhythm band was my best teacher. I look back and see a girl with a wide grin, straight brown hair pulled back in a ponytail. She's sitting in the back row playing those sticks with all her heart. And I wouldn't trade that place now for a hundred spotlights. It was good training for one who now plays the sticks in a larger rhythm band today: the carpool driver, the casserole fixer, the church-kitchen cleaner, the kisser of skinned knees. She is the keeper of the steady background beat that moves the world, the measure that makes life's music flow.

Thanks, God, for using the sticks to make me strong.
—Pam Kidd

*Thou art no more a servant, but a son; and . . . an heir of
God. . . .*   —Galatians 4:7

Back in my growing-up days in Kentucky, Felix
Drayton was the happiest boy I knew. I looked forward to
the times when he'd come out to play because he was
always fun, never sulking when he struck out or getting
mad when we teased him.

It used to puzzle me that Felix could be so happy even
though he was so poor. He wore patched clothes and he
never got to go to the movies on Saturday afternoon the
way we did, and his mama had to do housework for a
living, instead of being home with him.

The only thing wrong with Felix was that he was a
little stuck-up. In fact, it annoyed me considerably when
he would stare me straight in the face and tell me that he
was a prince. When I'd point out to him that he wasn't,
he'd just say firmly that he was, and then he'd pull himself
up and shamelessly repeat how he was "of royal blood."

"Mrs. Drayton," I said to his mama one day when I met
her on the street, "why does Felix think he's a prince?"

"Because he is," she replied serenely. "Felix is a prince,
same as you."

"Me?" I was astonished.

"Why sure. You're both children of God, aren't you?
You're sons of the King!"

We moved north a year or two after that. I've never
known what happened to Felix or how he's fared in life.
But when you grow up with the self-confidence of a
prince, as Felix did, I'm sure he went a long way. And I'll
bet he's still going.

Father, help me to live up to my own regal birthright.
                                                      —Van Varner

LESSONS OF TIME
❧❧❧

Every day is a gift. We dread the passing years, yet enjoy each day as it comes. We value our time on earth because it is limited. But we learn new things daily and can enjoy the perspective we gain. We can live our lives fully and joyfully because we are growing and learning and we know that we will have a new life after this earthly one.

In this section, you'll see how some people enjoy life instead of looking back and in some cultures, you will be venerated for your wisdom when you are 70! That's something to look forward to.

To every thing there is a season.

—ECCLESIASTES 3:1

FOR THE YEARS AHEAD

Another year!
Please help me, Lord!
I'm growing old and there's so much yet
  to do.
Last year seems such a short time ago;
Yet, when I think of all the blessings,
the new friends and experiences,
opportunities to work the clay
with new techniques, deeper insights—
Then I'm mindful of the ways in which
You've helped me grow.
And my heart looks forward to the years
  ahead.

—Jacki Keck

Let us lay aside every weight. . . .   —Hebrews 12:1

🎣 **My** husband's 50th high school reunion in Vancouver, British Columbia has come and gone. I could not go with him, so our son took my place. "Make sure your dad has a good time," I told Ian.

But when John and I went over his senior yearbook before they left, I wondered whether he would have a good time. "Here's Colleen," John said wistfully. "I was sweet on her but I couldn't get up the nerve to ask her for a date. And this fellow here," John's voice was tense, "he belonged to a club they wouldn't let me join."

"Where's your picture?" I asked, puzzled.

"It's here at the end. I wasn't sure I could cough up the extra money for a picture until the last minute."

His picture didn't show up in any other section except with the air cadets. "I wasn't one of the popular bunch. If Ian wasn't coming, I don't think I'd go."

Three days later the fellows returned, loaded with pictures and autographed programs. "Honey, I wouldn't have missed it for the world!" John said excitedly. "Colleen was there at our table. She said she always liked me and would have dated me if I'd asked! The chaps I thought had shut me out–thought I was a brain and knew I would do well without the group's help. I've spent a lifetime brooding about what I thought was the rejection of my classmates. Turns out that every ounce of that burden I put on myself. This week at the reunion, I threw the weight of it off!"

"Thanks be to God," I said as I kissed him.

Dear Lord, help us to throw off the weights from our past that we have carried all our lives, and to forgive ourselves and others.
                                                          —Fay Angus

In my Father's house there are many mansions. . . —John 14:2

🍃 As a boy, I heard many stories about "the Old Gaz Place" where my father and his brothers and sisters grew up. Now at age 44 on a visit back to Georgia, I stood with my mother and father in the weed-filled driveway of the Gaz Place for the first time.

The ramshackle old house was boarded up, but we found an unboarded door and crept into the room that had been the kitchen, "Through this door is the living room," Dad said as he led the way. A small riverstone fireplace flattened itself against one wall. On the opposite side, a door opened to the only other room. "This is the bedroom were all six of us children slept." The room was tiny.

"Dad, there's hardly enough room for a bed."

"We had three," he said. "Our parents slept out in the living room."

I tried to imagine my wife and me and our three children living in the small space. *Impossible!* I thought.

Three tiny rooms, yet room enough for all. From the tiny Gaz Place and its lessons in sharing limited space and unlimited love, my father has gone on to live a life full of sharing. He worked for more than 38 years in a hospital caring for the sick, coached Little League baseball, and taught Sunday school to countless youngsters who are now adults and are multiplying his gift by doing the same.

Thanks to my visit to the Gaz Place, I've been reminded that a humble start does not necessarily result in a limited life. And when I sometimes think, *If I had more, I'd do more*, I remember my visit to "the Old Gaz Place." *I've got plenty*, I tell myself. *All I need to do is use it.*

Father, help me to appreciate what I have, and to share
generously out of my plenty.   —John Bramblett

Bless the Lord, O my soul, and forget not all his benefits . . .
who satisfieth thy mouth with good things; so that thy youth is
renewed like the eagle's. —Psalm 103:2, 5

"Start each day with a full cup."

That's the advice that was offered recently by a woman in my Bible study group. She went on the explain that for her, "filling the cup" means spending time each morning in prayer and fellowship with God, then eating a nourishing breakfast, bathing, dressing well, and taking special care with her hair and makeup.

"If I don't do all those things, then a nagging feeling of dissatisfaction affects my attitude and my work all day long," she said. "But if I get those things taken care of, then my cup is full. I can forget about myself and concentrate on my work, the day, the people around me. I live that day in God's fullness."

Maybe it seems as though everyone would logically start the day that way, but I know many people who are unemployed or retired or who conduct their business at home, as I do. And I confess from experience that it's a temptation to postpone the grooming, the breakfast, the prayer time with God, if you're not bound by an outside office schedule. But ever since that Bible study class, I've made myself stick to a regimen of self-discipline that covers, first thing in the day, all the areas my friend mentioned, with God at the top of the list.

And my friend is right. When my cup is full, I work better, and I reach out with confidence to those who come my way.

Father, here is my cup. Please fill it with Your Presence.
—*Madge Harrah*

❧ **S**ome of life's best gifts have come to me in small, undramatic moments, like the words that came shortly after I began my first job from a woman whom I never saw.

"I hear you are working with the old folks at the county home," said a voice on the telephone. "I want to help. Write down my number and when one of those dear people has a need, you are to call and let me know. In the meantime, I'll be checking back with you."

At least once or twice a week my morning would begin with one of her calls. If I knew someone who needed a new coat, or a special book, or the comfort of a soft stuffed animal, all I had to do was ask. She was a self-appointed link among local churches, civic groups, caring individuals, and people in need.

We had many telephone conversations before I learned that she was an invalid, confined to her bed. I was astounded. "How can you think of others, when you have so many problems yourself?"

"My dear, in the first year of my confinement I spent all my time feeling sorry for myself, until a very wise friend said to me, 'What's happened has happened. You can face it with bitterness, or you can face it with grace."

"Moving the center of attention from myself to others, I found I could use the telephone to perform at least one useful act each day. One act of kindness blossomed into two, then three," she continued, "and now my days are full. When I wake up, I say, 'This is a new day. Face it with grace,' just to remind myself what I'm about."

Today her words continue to bless me. To face the day means no regrets from the past, no resentments in the present, no fears of the future. It is to say each morning:

What can I do for You today, God?   *—Pam Kidd*

. . . Not by might, not by power, but by my spirit, saith the
Lord of hosts. —Zechariah 4:6

After my husband died, I had to learn to do things I'd never done before. I did pretty well buying a new furnace, having the house painted, buying tires for the car, and I'm still working on balancing the checkbook. But recently I had to face something that was the toughest thing of all.

The faucet in the kitchen dripped–constantly. For three weeks I'd wake up at three in the morning and hear it and wonder: *What will I do about that faucet?* I finally phoned a plumber and he said it would be $50 just for a house call. I was convinced it was something simple–I just didn't know what. I was awake again the next night. *Lord, I don't know what to do, but I'm starting to be afraid of the faucet. Help me.*

Late the next afternoon I was seized with the strange idea that I could fix the faucet! I was stunned, but excited. Determined, I made three trips to the hardware store, each time taking a different piece of the faucet. All five employees helped me. "You've got more nerve that any woman I ever met," one of the men helping me mumbled. Greatly encouraged, I smiled all the way home. I put in a little washer not much thicker than a rubber band. The trick was getting to where the washer belonged and replacing all that "stuff." But I fixed the leak! Washers are magnificent little things. I had a regular celebration in the kitchen when I turned the faucet off and not one tiny drop went plop.

Is there something you're afraid to try? Seek His help–your problem may be "washer" simple!

Don't let me forget, Father, that by Your spirit, I can do all
kinds of things. —Marion Bond West

*For by grace are ye saved through faith; and that not of
yourselves; it is the gift of God.*   —Ephesians 2:8

Attending a religious gathering, I became increasing-
ly uncomfortable. I was getting the impression that everyone at that meeting spent long hours reading the Bible and
praying, and devoted their weekends to selfless deeds of
love and mercy. Everyone seemed free from sin, with all
personal struggles neatly wrapped up somewhere in the
past. But I knew that I wasn't that good, that virtuous, or
that holy. I was still very human with lots of faults and
plenty of doubts, and I didn't measure up to any 24-hour-
a-day standard of piety.

But I was also aware that, though my feelings of unwor-
thiness at the moment were real, I was being ridiculous. I
knew a lot of the people at the gathering personally. They
too are human. They struggle with sin. They struggle for
faith. Yet somehow that didn't help my feelings.

Perhaps that is why the words of an older pastor struck
a chord with me: "I give God thanks today for something
my daddy said to me. He was an old Ozark farmer and
spoke his mind. He said, 'Don't you never forget, boy, that
God can hit a pretty straight lick with a mighty crooked
stick.' I guess if Daddy hadn't told me that, I could never
have stayed in the ministry these 30 years."

These folksy words made me smile. *Of course!* I thought.
*God isn't waiting for me to become perfect before He's going to use me.
He uses ordinary people—like me—to do His work, to love others in His
name. If this weren't so, we'd all be in deep trouble.*

I took a deep breath and relaxed. Thanks to God's grace,
it is okay to be a "crooked stick."

*Father, help me to accept myself as You accept me, and to hit a
"straight lick" in Your world.*   —Scott Walker

Let us therefore come boldly unto the throne . . . that we may . . .
find grace to help in time of need.   —Hebrews 4:16

☙Talking on the telephone to Mary, a dear friend, I was
surprised to hear her say, "I've never been anywhere. I've
never traveled. Actually, I've only been to a few southern
states here near Georgia. I'd like to see the Grand Canyon,
the giant redwoods, . . . so many places. I'd like to be able
to travel. . . . " There was an unmistakable note of sadness
in her voice. Then she quickly moved on to another topic.

Her confession touched me. I'd rarely known my friend
to complain or ask for more than was hers. So I spoke to
God about it. "Show me a way to encourage her, Father,"
I prayed. "She's encouraged so many—including me." I
waited, listening with my heart. The thought that came
was so gentle and unobtrusive that I almost held my
breath so I wouldn't miss it. I wrote down what I thought
I had heard and called my friend. "I think God has told me
something about your longing to travel. Would you like to
hear it?"

"Well, sure." I could tell, even on the telephone, that she
smiled.

"I believe He said that you've been to His Throne Room
many, many times—in intercession for others. He seemed
to say that the room isn't crowded at all and that He's glad
to have you travel there often and pray before Him."

Silence. A very long silence. "Thank you," a joyful voice
said.

My greatest longing, Lord—one that is always satisfied by
You—is to travel faithfully every day to Your Throne Room
and intercede for others through the marvelous vehicle of prayer.
Here are those special ones today: —Marion Bond West

When I became a man, I put away childish things.
—*I Corinthians* 13:11

I turned 40 this year, and it wasn't the crisis it was supposed to be. All around me friends were having birthday parties with black balloons and gifts like hair restorer, denture cream, and Ben-Gay. Me? I couldn't wait for the day. And I've decided to let you know my secret.

Ten years ago I visited a church in Hong Kong where, after the service, they had a big party for the man who'd preached the sermon. They were celebrating his 40th birthday. Following the party was another service of some sort, very solemn and proper. I learned that the preacher was being ordained. In their culture, a male is not fully a man until he turns 40 and therefore cannot take the final rites of ordination until that birthday arrives.

Right there I decided to adopt the Chinese approach to aging, which made the day something to be anticipated, not dreaded. By the way, the Chinese have another big birthday party when you turn 70. Then you become venerated and sought after for your wisdom. I can't wait!

Lord, thank You for every birthday and for the experience, grace, and wisdom that each year brings. —*Eric Fellman*

For I know whom I have believed, and am persuaded that he is able to keep that which I have committed unto him against that day.
—II Timothy 1:12

❧ Recently I read a story about Bernard Topel, an Episcopalian minister known for his great faith. After his retirement, Bishop Topel's mind began to fail and he was moved to a nursing home.

Shortly before his death a reporter went to interview him. It was a painful experience. Bishop Topel couldn't discuss theology. He didn't remember events that had taken place while he was bishop of Spokane. He even forgot the names of his friends. Finally the writer said, trying to be sympathetic, "It's hard to get old, isn't it?"

Bishop Topel looked out the window for a long time. Then he turned to the writer and said quietly, "All my life I have given everything to God. If God wants my mind, He can have that, too."

The bishop had a depth of commitment that allowed him to accept the changing circumstances of his life. He trusted God completely, and that trust gave him the courage to face life . . . and death.

All to Jesus I surrender,
All to Him I freely give.
I will ever love and trust Him,
In His presence daily live.

Amen.

Father, grant me the courage to trust You in all things.
—Penney Schwab

71

Shall the thing formed say to him that formed it, Why hast thou made me thus?
—Romans 9:20

🍃 I picked up a book and started reading about James Naismith. In the 1880s, he spent three years in a seminary but never became a pastor. He earned a medical degree but never practiced. As a teacher at the YMCA Training School in Springfield, Massachusetts, he invented a game he hoped would hold his students' interest. With a soccer ball and a couple of peach baskets nailed to the balcony above the hardwood floor, Dr. Naismith invented basketball.

I'm intrigued by his story. He didn't become what he set out to be. His life moved in an entirely different direction from what he had planned. I can't help but think of the direction my own life has taken. I'm not starring in a Broadway musical or hosting a morning talk show. Those were dreams for me at one time. But God led me in other directions. Some days I wonder what might have been, but I can't say I'm disappointed. God knew that marriage and children were in my dreams, too, and those have come true beautifully.

I'm trying to imagine where God's plan for me is headed. That's where the second and even more intriguing aspect of Dr. Naismith's story comes to mind. When "The Father of Basketball" died in 1939 at age 78, he had no idea what he had created. Like Dr. Naismith, I may never know how what I've done reaches into the future, but God does. On days when I can't see beyond the end of my driveway, I'm comforted by this: God knows well the road I'm on because He set me on it, and He knows where I'm heading because He's leading me there.

God, light my way along Your path so that all I do leads me toward the destination You have in mind. —Gina Bridgeman

The French author Henri Etienne has said that God tempers the wind to the shorn lamb. I suppose we have all felt like shorn lambs at times, defenseless against the rough winds that blow on us.

I know I have felt most "shorn" in the physical area. As I get older, I feel almost defenseless against the creeping loss of energy, but I have become aware of God's compensations. I have lost the energy of youth, but I have gained the patience to wait for things to come my way. I have lost the physical ability I once had, but since I am not always on the run, I am able to set aside an hour each day for reflection and meditation. I have had to retire from my chosen occupation, but I have gained the opportunity to take up woodworking and to develop my musical talent.

Every loss is tempered by a gain if only we have the eyes to see and the heart to pursue. God's promises and blessings are not given only to the young and the strong; they are even more precious to the "shorn lambs."

Dear Lord, today I want to focus on my compensations, not on my limitations. For this, I will need your help, and I thank You in advance for it. Amen. —Lee Webber

No man also having drunk old wine straightway desireth new: for he saith, The old is better. —Luke 5:39

I'm 50 years old today. This is the age that was always a long way off in my future, the age I've never imagined being because somewhere in the dim recesses of my mind, 50 has always been the end of "young" and the beginning of "old."

This morning I noticed–for the first time–that my makeup routine seems to take a lot longer lately, and the result is not what it used to be. Worse, the extra pounds I was always able to peel off with a quick diet now seem cemented to my body–in all the most obvious and undisguisable places. I try to remember who it was who said that, "After 50, it's patch, patch, patch," but her name escapes me. (Unfortunately, my memory has become a sieve in the last few years.)

Still, I remind myself, there *are* advantages to having survived 50 years. By now I've made most of the worst mistakes a human being can make, so I hope I won't repeat them. I've also learned the priceless lessons only time can teach–lessons that make life *infinitely* better at 50 than at 20 or 30: things usually *do* look better in the morning, no letter written in the heat of emotion should be mailed for at least 24 hours, it's easier to forgive the sins of an enemy than those of a spouse, *everything* in this world is temporary, nobody I admire has had an easier life than I have, and God is the only One Who will not disappoint me if I expect Him to be perfect.

Would I trade knowledge like this for a younger face or body? Come to think of it, no.

Okay, Lord, I'll buy it. Older is better. —Susan Williams

O Lord, thou hast searched me, and known me. —Psalm 139:1

&❧ On the June morning 30 years ago when my son was put into my arms, I waited until the nurse was out of the room and then, my eye still on the door, I pulled loose the deftly bound blanket and began to examine the tiny person it had hidden.

He seemed perfect to me, even the crooked little toes, so like his father's large ones. I marveled, as any new mother might, that this wonderful child had grown for these past nine months inside my body.

And I wasn't the only one. Everyone thought he was beautiful. Why, the first words the nurse had said in the delivery room were, "Look at those eyelashes! Wouldn't you know? Wasted on a boy."

Someday I thought, stroking his silky cheek, *someday, he's going to have to shave.* I laughed aloud at the thought.

The psalmist remembers that same wonder over the creation of a person when he says in Psalm 139:13-14: "For thou hast possessed my reins: thou hast covered me in my mother's womb. I will praise thee: for I am fearfully and wonderfully made. . . . "

As I read the Psalm this morning, I see the Parent of us all bending in love over me. And I see that the marvel we share in God's creation is nothing new. Yet it is new for every parent at every birth. God not only made me, God loves me, searching me with the eyes of a love-struck mother marveling over her newborn child.

Let me know, O God, Your tender searching love that awakens in me the desire for You.
—Katherine Paterson

Lord, thou hast been our dwelling place in all generations.
                                                    —Psalm 90:1

🌿 It was my mother's 83rd birthday and I was not looking forward to visiting her. She no longer could say for
sure what year she was born. In the 1950s she had been a
quiz show champion.

On the drive to the home where my siblings and I had
moved her, my own memory troubled me. I thought of all
the times she had wanted me to visit and I hadn't.

I was in a bad state when I arrived at the group home,
though the fierce strength of her hug was a surprise coming from the stooped figure who greeted me. "My
youngest," she announced. We sat together on the porch
for a time when, suddenly, Mom said, "Remember my
birthday when you played the trombone?"

I thought she was drifting into some irritating absurdity,
and then a memory fell open. I must have been about
nine, and I'd just taken up the trombone. It was a sad time.
We'd lost my brother in a tragic death, my older sister and
other brother were off to college, and my father was away.
Just the two of us were celebrating with one candle and a
little cake.

"Until you came down the stairs playing 'Happy
Birthday' on your trombone, it was the worst birthday of
my life. Now I think it might have been the best."

As my mother relapsed into silence, my bad state began
to turn. *God makes certain memories strong for us,* I thought, *so
that when our capacity to remember begins to fail, the best can still pre-
vail for those times we need them most.* I felt a warm strength flow
in the hug that came from my mother's frail and brittle
arms. It is the strength of the spirit when the body fails,
and of God bringing out the best in us.

*God, help me not to dwell on my failings, but to build on the
love and goodness in my life.*   *—Edward Grinnan*

LIFE LESSONS
꙰

There is nothing more annoying than a "learning experience." That phrase is usually attached to some unpleasant, usually unplanned event. You might try to do something too difficult in order to impress other people. You could avoid something as simple as drawing a picture because you're not good enough.

As you read these pieces, you'll see we've all got a lot to learn—but we can be as good as we need to be. All God wants us to be is ourselves. Now that's a lesson that's easy to learn.

Happy is the man that findeth wisdom.

—PROVERBS 3:13

THROUGH THE YEARS

Dear God,
I understand that we age from the moment
we are born,
but as the years add up I sometimes question
whether I've
accomplished all I can in this lifetime.

Help me to see through clear eyes
the visions of hope left to accomplish.

Help me to hear through keen ears
the words of wisdom to be spoken.

Help me know with a youthful heart
the desires and dreams yet to achieve.

Let me see the grace, mercy, forgiveness
and knowledge as I look in the mirror.
For what are we if not a reflection of you?
    Amen.

                    —Carla Flack

Whatsoever ye do, do all to the glory of God.
—*I Corinthians* 10:31

🌺 "**W**e've had a sudden change in plans and I'm wondering if you can help out." It was our pastor on the telephone. "Can you host the guest soloist and her husband for lunch after church tomorrow?"

I gasped inwardly as I looked around the kitchen. We'd been tending to an abundant crop of vegetables from our garden, and our four kids had all been "helping," as evidenced by a trail of empty pea pods leading to the television and carrot tops strewn about on the counter. Having company tomorrow would necessitate a major cleanup campaign *today*.

I was about to say no when I remembered the sermon from last Sunday about showing hospitality to strangers. "Yes, Pastor, I think we can manage it," I responded.

Hastily, I finished the pickling, then mopped, tidied, dusted, and vacuumed the entire house. *What a lot of trouble that was just for them,* I thought as I collapsed. *I hope it's worth it.*

The next morning at church I found that our guests were good friends. And they are both *blind!*

I needn't have gone to all that trouble! I told myself during church. Later, we all had a good chuckle about the futility of my cleanup efforts when they couldn't be seen anyway.

"Oh, but I can *smell* the difference," Gail declared.

Her comment has never left me. It reminds me that although much of my work may be behind the scenes, the results are almost always proportionate to the time and effort I expend. And perceptive people can "smell" the difference.

Father, thank You that You see and appreciate whatever I do for You, however small. Help me always to do it to the best of my abilities.
—*Alma Barkman*

Let every man prove his own work, and then shall he have
rejoicing in himself alone and not in another. . . . For every man
shall bear his own burden.   —Galatians 6:4-5

🐝 Do you compare yourself unfavorably to others? I often do. To make matters worse, I'm a competitive person. On the one hand I feel inferior, and on the other hand I feel driven to prove myself better.

An example of this internal warring occurred when my church asked me to help with their annual pledge drive. Volunteers would chat with each family, discuss pertinent Bible passages, share a prayer, and receive the sealed pledge. I panicked when I heard who'd already volunteered. *Hal, Marion, Diane, George.* "I can't possibly measure up to them," I wailed. "They're just naturally good at such things."

While I was searching desperately for a graceful way to refuse, I came across an article about John Wooden, the basketball coach who led UCLA to ten NCAA championships. The reporter asked him how he motivated his players. "I tell them, 'Don't try to be better than someone else. Be the best you can be. Nobody's better than that.'"

Well, I thought, *if it worked for Coach Wooden. . . .* I didn't exactly breeze through those family meetings. Each one presented a palm-sweating challenge. But I did the best I could. And afterward I felt at peace with myself, because I realized that was all God ever expected in the first place.

Are you bending over backward trying to be as good as someone else? Try being as good as you can be. It's a lot more productive.

Lord, You created me. Help me to be all You want me to be.
                                            —Bonnie Lukes

We have done that which was our duty to do. —Luke 17:10

The heavy wooden drawer in our kitchen holds a thousand pairs of pot holders. Only one pair works!

Whenever I'm popping my usual evening popcorn, I reach for the blue pot holders with the white ducks on them because they are perfect.

Some of the potholders are too big–they droop down and catch on fire. Some pot holders are too thin and offer little protection. Some are thick and stiff, and I can't get a good grip with them.

So I use the blue ones, against my wife's protests, because they work.

The blue pot holders remind me that perhaps the greatest test of worth is the practical test. When I go into the classroom to teach, no one cares about my degrees, or my poor memory, or my crooked tie. The important thing is that I can teach. I may not be the best teacher, but I'm not the worst, either. I do the job faithfully, and I seldom miss a class.

What about you? So what if you aren't the most qualified worker in your shop? So what if you aren't the most attractive-looking spouse? What does it matter if you aren't the star of the team? *Can you do the job?* Then give yourself a pat on the back, because you have passed one of the most stringent tests of all–the test of practicality.

Just do it.

Lord, I may not be the best, but I'm available and willing. Use me.
—*Daniel Schantz*

In the world ye shall have tribulation: but be of good cheer; I have overcome the world. —John 16:33

When I remember Martin Luther King, Jr., I envision him as he appeared in many photographs while singing "We Shall Overcome." And then I recall another, very different occasion when that song became my theme song, too.

It was 1969. Uganda had become an independent African nation. I was visiting a deaf children's school in its capital city Kampala. All the students there, were from poor families. Buying a hearing aid for their one deaf child was beyond their reach, so the deaf child had to rely on what little hearing he or she might possess. Some did learn lipreading, a few managed to complete their education.

During my visit the children shyly lined up to sing for me. They'd been told that I was an American with a hearing impairment like their own and, with the help of two hearing aids, I could hear them. They began singing in Swahili, which I didn't understand at first. After a few refrains, I began to recognize the tune: "We shall overcome, We shall overcome. . . ." Suddenly, it became more than a civil rights song. Impulsively, I moved to clasp the hand of the last child in line and to sing along with them. As I did, the children's smiles told me that they, too, understood the double meaning of the words.

Two days later, as my plane took off from Kampala for the United States, I stared out the window at the lush, green landscape below. And I said this prayer.

Father, all of Your children have handicaps of one kind or another. Give us courage and strength to overcome them.
—Eleanor Sass

For charity [love] shall cover the multitude of sins.
—I Peter 4:8

&❧ Whenever I go to a formal party or banquet, I get a knot in my stomach. And it's not from the food. I guess it sounds silly, but I'm unsure of my etiquette. Sometimes I don't know what to do or say.

Recently, a friend taught me to relax. "Etiquette was invented to carry out the Golden Rule," he pointed out. "Kindness came before the rules. Just do the loving thing and you will be fairly safe," he added.

I still have times when I don't know what to do: which fork to use first, what to say when introducing someone, how to leave a social gathering gracefully. I've stopped trying so hard to be "correct," and I concentrate on being gracious.

The Golden Rule is the one rule that supersedes all our trivial and tedious traditions, or so it seems to me. When I don't know what to wear to a reception, I ask myself, "What is modest? What would make others feel good and not steal the show?" When I'm pondering a wedding gift purchase, instead of asking, "What should I spend?" or "What would impress?" I ask myself, "What do the newly-weds need?" Then there are those two big-little phrases that are always correct: "Please" and "Thank you."

Love. It covers a multitude of gaffes.

Father, when I know not what to do, teach me always to love.
—Daniel Schantz

But we all, with open face beholding as in a glass the glory of the Lord, are changed into the same image. . .
—II Corinthians 3:18

People who come into my art studio often ask me, "What is your most helpful tool?" They wonder, *Is it the brush? The easel? The tube of white?* To their surprise, I point to the mirror in front of my easel.

When I am laboring deeply and happily on a painting, I can become so engrossed in what I'm doing that although the painting looks right as it sits in front of me, something may be very wrong. My staring and concentration actually rob me of objectivity. But if I look at my painting in the mirror, the flaw will pop out. It's like seeing it through another's fresh eyes! I can see what's wrong and make the correction.

I have another frank, honest mirror: my Bible. I couldn't do without its telling reflections. The tendency to become inwardly focused and think, *I'm not so bad. Why I'm just as good as so-and-so* is jolted by II Corinthians 10:12 warning against comparative bragging: "We dare not make ourselves of the number, or compare ourselves with some that commend themselves. . . ."

By contrast, my "God doesn't care about little old me" is proven out of perspective when held to the loving mirror of I John 4:10: "He loved us, and sent his Son to be the propitiation for our sins."

The mirror's truth sometimes hurts. It means backing up and starting again. But I can't make the corrections if I don't know where the problem is. Artwork or life, I need my mirrors.

Dear Lord, let the mirror of Your Word do its work, that my life might reflect You.
—Kathie Kania

Ye have need of patience. . . .   —*Hebrews* 10:36

❧ What is there to show for your life? Or rather, what isn't there to show for it. I pondered this after reading about Dr. Frances Kelsey.

Her name appeared in an article about thalidomide, the drug now associated with an epidemic of birth defects in Europe in the 1960s. Thalidomide was already being widely used in other countries when its manufacturer applied to the United States for permission to sell it here, and Dr. Kelsey was assigned to handle the application. She had reservations about thalidomide. The drug company tried to pressure her for approval, but she held her ground, insisting on more data. When some deformed European babies were traced to their mothers' taking thalidomide during pregnancy, the manufacturer dropped its application.

Although Dr. Kelsey subsequently received an award for her service, she remains a largely unsung heroine. I think that's because the world remembers what you produce, not what you prevent. Do you ever feel discouraged because you haven't written a book or painted a picture or patented an invention? Look at the other side of the coin. What about the borderline student you helped, who might have become a dropout? What about your hard work to instill good values in your children and other young people? Only God knows what you're preventing—an alcoholic, a drug addict, a suicide, a teenage pregnancy—but that's more than enough reward.

Dr. Frances Kelsey's legacy is young American men and women with whole arms and legs. She was a great preventer of tragedy. Maybe in some quiet way, you are one, too.

Lord, let me make a difference—visible or invisible.

                               —*B. J. Connor*

*I have nourished and brought up children, and they have
rebelled against me.*   *—Isaiah* 1:2

&❧ When I was 42 years old, I had my first experience
with motherhood: I married a man with two children—a
boy, 11, and a girl, 14. I'd like to report that we quickly
became a happy family, but it didn't work out that way. It
seemed that no matter what their father or I wanted, they
invariably wanted the opposite. But I was optimistic.
"What children need is lots of love and prayer," I told
myself. But even that solution didn't work. Unfortunately,
I felt more and more *responsible* for my stepchildren.

Then one day, something happened that turned things
around for me. It didn't change the children, mind you, or
even the situation—it just put things in perspective and
helped me stop blaming myself for being a failure as a parent.

What was it? The first three chapters of Genesis! They
told me that God—the model Father, the ideal Parent Who
can't make a mistake—brought two children into a perfect
world. He did *everything* right, but it wasn't enough to turn
Adam and Eve into the children He'd hoped they'd be.
They rebelled, choosing their own way instead of His.

What a comfort this was! The story of Adam and Eve
not only helped me accept my limitations as a parent, it
also taught me how to respond: as God did—with love,
patience, and forgiveness.

Are you trying too hard? Carrying the weight of the
world on your shoulders? Ease up, and ease God into the
picture. Then love, give, be the best human you can
possible be. Trust God to make up the difference.

*Father, I've been carrying to much. Let me be the most loving I
can be, and give the impossible to You.*   *—Susan Williams*

Hope deferred maketh the heart sick, but when the desire cometh, it is a tree of life. —Proverbs 13:12

A little while ago my doctor prescribed for me some strong medicine for my heart condition. As I read about this new medicine, I found that it could cause depression and even suicidal tendencies. The instructions even said that if suicidal tendencies develop, the medicine should be discontinued. Well, I should hope so!

I'm normally an optimist, but the medicine created a negative reaction in me. I found myself dredging up some negative experiences from the past; I also worried about my health. Finally, I got so depressed that I got down on my knees and said, "God, I have to fight back, I know. You don't want me to live like this. Please help me."

The next day I decided to try a new approach. I'd do positive things to crowd out the negative feelings. So, every day, I made time to listen to good music, to read a good book or informative article, to work on some interesting projects, and to get some good exercise. But most importantly, every day I took time to read the Word of God and pray. And slowly I began to find that despite the medication, I could control the down effects.

Do you struggle with depression or a habit that is causing you bad health? There are things you can do. First, get professional counseling. And then make up a series of steps that reinforce what makes you glad to be alive. Force yourself to enjoy life. And see how much you can make your own happiness—with God's help.

Dear Lord, help me to shut the door on dark and negative things, and open the windows of my mind to the sunlight of beautiful things. Amen. —Lee Webber

Whosoever therefore shall confess me before men, him will I confess also before my Father which is in heaven.
—Matthew 10:32

My husband and I were fulfilling a lifelong vacation dream in Hawaii. It was everything we'd imagined, although I soon wearied of the constant barrage of exuberant *Alohas!*

Just when I thought I couldn't stand to hear one more sweet-smiling "Aloha!" we met Wayne, a native Hawaiian. I was surprised when he greeted us softly. "'Aloha' means the presence of the Spiritual One and should never be shouted," he said. He explained that when Hawaiian children greet their parents in the morning with a reverently spoken "Aloha," they are saying, "May you be in the presence of the Holy One this day."

"The Holy One," Wayne added very matter-of-factly. "is, of course, Jesus Christ."

I was impressed by the courage of his public declaration of faith. At the same time, I was uncomfortably reminded of how often I monitor my own speech when I'm around strangers, softening the religious words lest I be thought overzealous. Remembering made me cringe over such cowardly behavior. I'd never felt the sting so sharply as when Wayne so simply and elegantly acknowledged the Savior to a busload of strangers.

I bowed my head and promised God that the next time I caught myself trying to be "cool," hiding my faith "under a bushel," I'd remember Wayne and follow his faithful example.

Thank you, Father, for placing courageous and faithful disciples in my path, that I might take strength from them in living my faith publicly as naturally as I do privately.
—Bonnie Lukes

In all things shewing thyself a pattern of good works. . . .
                                                    —*Titus* 2:7

I signed up for duty at a children's hospital in Manhattan with hopes of saving the world—only to discover I was the world's worst volunteer. Every Tuesday night, I joined 20 other women to lead craft time for young kids who lived at the hospital year round. My sheltered, Alabama childhood had certainly not prepared me to work with city kids from broken homes. I colored and painted with them, but their emotional outbreaks and battles for our attention made me a nervous wreck. I didn't know how to reach out to them—even hugging was against the rules because most of the children had been abused. After a few months of failing to connect, I was just about ready to give up. Surely someone else could love them better than I.

On what was to have been my last night, eight-year-old Victor wanted help drawing a tiger. "Please, somebody," he pleaded, as one by one the volunteers turned him down. "How about you?" He stood right in front of me with a brown crayon. I didn't want him to be disappointed, but it was only fair to warn him: "It won't be perfect, Victor."

He frowned and pointed right between my eyes. "Nothing in life is perfect, but you have to try." I looked at that child, whose life had been anything but perfect, and knew he was right. I might never be the best volunteer, but I could be a willing one. So I tried. And for weeks to come, a goofy tiger with a lopsided grin hung over my favorite second-grader's bed.

Lord, I know I'm not perfect, but with my trust in You, I'll try.
                                                    —*Allison Sample*

*Let all bitterness, and wrath, and anger, and clamor, and evil
speaking, be put away from you. . . .*   —*Ephesians* 4:31

🔊 It was a beautiful spring day with a clear blue sky, a
few fluffy white clouds, and a lively breeze. A perfect
day–except for people like me with allergies. Pollen was
blowing in the wind, I had the runny nose and swollen
eyes to prove it, and I felt miserable.

I was walking my dog along our road, eager to get back
home, when I saw Don Evans, a teacher friend, out for his
morning jog. As he approached, he grinned, waved, and
said, "Great day, isn't it?"

"Not if you can't breath," was what I was going to say,
but I hesitated. Don was in a happy mood. Why spoil it
with a sour remark? Somehow, I didn't want to be the kind
of person who would do that. So I grinned back and said,
"Have fun!" Immediately, my own spirits lifted.

I can't count the times I have allowed my bad moods to
spill over into other people's lives. But when I do that, I
don't like myself. My brief encounter with Don showed
me that I can choose the kind of person I want to be.
When I'm in a bad mood, I can try a little harder to consider the feelings of those around me. I can ask myself, *Do
I want to spoil their day or make it nicer?* It all comes down to a
pretty simple choice: What kind of a person do I want to
be?

*Lord, help me to choose, even in the hard times, to be a
spirit-lifter.*   —*Phyllis Hobe*

Lord I believe; help thou mine unbelief.   —Mark 9:24

They call it "Chicken Rock" because half the people who climb to the top of the rock to jump off into the water "chicken out." Staring up at it, I watched my boys climb to the top. It seemed incredibly high, so I called out, "You guys can just call me 'Mr. Chicken.'" But after showing me a dozen carefree leaps into the lake, they finally coaxed me to the top.

It was an interesting exercise. I couldn't get myself over the edge. My mind said it could be done—my boys proved it—yet I couldn't do it. Finally one of them said to me, "C'mon, Dad. You've got to have faith." So I jumped.

It was incredible—the rush of fear pushed aside by the exhilaration of falling and the relief of popping up safely. One jump broke the barrier, and now I can show other "chickens" how it's done.

The exercise of faith in my spiritual life has a similar pattern. Last fall an outburst from a coworker caused hurt among several people. I knew the faith-filled response would be to confront the person lovingly. But "Mr. Chicken" wants to keep his head down and wait for the storm to pass.

Or more recently, I was selected to approach the head of a large corporation for a donation. "Mr. Chicken" wanted to shake his hand, leave the brochure, and let him "think about it." By leaping out in faith, I was able to say, "We'd like you to consider giving $100,000."

In both cases, I took the leap. Nothing can compare with the joy of finding a deeper friendship out of hurt and the thanksgiving of receiving a generous donation.

Are you standing at the top of "Chicken Rock" today? Leap out. You will not be disappointed.

Lord, keep me leaping!   —Eric Fellman

Remember now thy Creator in the days of thy youth. . . .
—Ecclesiastes 12:1

❧ Tim was almost 13, awkward and shy. He hadn't gone to the pool or biked around town with his pals that summer.

So when he left home in late July for Boy Scout camp, my heart ached. There was nothing he could do at camp that wasn't intensely physical and competitive. From the very first event–the swim test that qualified a scout for all the waterfront activities–he would have to pit his courage and abilities against other, bigger boys.

Then his first letter, "Yesterday, I had to swim 100 meters using four different strokes. I knew I couldn't hold out without my lungs bursting, so I sat on the porch of the lifeguard's hut to wait my turn. I still didn't know if I'd try, but then I saw something on the wall. A photo of a race and this verse: 'I can do all things through Christ which strengtheneth me' (Philippians 4:13).

I decided then to go ahead with it, and when it came to my turn, I repeated the verse inside my head as I swam. It was hard, but I PASSED! I PASSED!"

He was learning to sail, and to survive "in the middle of nowhere without so much as a knife." He returned, tanned and with poison ivy, belting out camp songs in a voice that would sometimes hit unexpected deep notes.

He had gone away that summer to face some new challenges alone. He'd returned, a little grown up, with new self-confidence–and a renewed faith in God that told him he would never be alone again.

Remind us never to be afraid to try, Heavenly Father, for Your strength and protection can carry us past all obstacles.
—Linda Ching Sledge

Lift up your eyes. . . .   —*Isaiah* 40:26

"**W**ant to take an after-dinner walk?" my husband David asks.

In my best martyred-fishwife voice I answer, "With half the house left to clean? To further make my point, I yell down the hall. "Brock! Keri! Don't even think of going to bed until your rooms are cleaned!"

"Oh, Mama," Keri, then six, replies, "we were going to catch lightening bugs."

An hour later, I scan my "things-to-do" list, and see that like last week and the week before, the house is reasonably clean. *Oops, the porch.* Broom in hand, I open the door. The whirr of the vacuum and flying dust have dulled my senses. But one whiff of summer and I'm in another time zone. I think of Keri's lightning bugs, and I recall childhood's cool grass under bare feet and the fresh watermelon smell. Later, the backyard glider would float like a boat adrift on a secret sea, as I watched luminous lights blinking, blinking, inside a jelly jar.

I walk across the porch, sit on the top step. In the simple dark I take stock. Do I really want my children to know me as a grouchy mom with a very clean house?

Summer was offering an alternative. I hurry inside, take four empty jars from under the sink and call my glum family of house-cleaners together. "I have a problem with lightening bugs," I say. "I need to see if it's still fun to catch them on a summer night." And then because confession brightens the soul, I add, "I think it might be more important than a clean house."

It was. It still is.

I'd rather be a lightning-bug chaser, Lord. Help me hold that vision.
                                                        —*Pam Kidd*

A Note from the Editors

The writers in this book write for *Daily Guideposts,* an annual devotional book published by Guideposts. This book was created by the Book and Inspirational Media Division of the company that publishes *Daily Guideposts* and *Guideposts,* a monthly magazine filled with true stories of hope and inspiration. Each month you can count on receiving exciting new evidence of God's presence, His guidance and His limitless love for all of us.

You can order either *Daily Guideposts* or *Guideposts* in regular or large print by writing to Guideposts, 39 Seminary Hill Road, Carmel, New York 10512.

Guideposts books are available on the World Wide Web at www.guidepostsbooks.com. Follow our popular book of devotionals, *Daily Guideposts,* and read excerpts from some of our best-selling books. You can also send prayer requests to our Monday morning Prayer Fellowship and read stories from recent issues of our magazines, *Guideposts, Angels on Earth,* and *Guideposts for Teens.*